SACRAMENT

"It's rare to read vibrant, witty, piercing essays that get waaay under the small boat of religion and deep into the sea of our wild spiritual search. It's a delight when you find essays like that from Barry Lopez and Annie Dillard, and it's a delight to find them here, from one of the best Catholic essayists in America."

Brian Doyle
Author of *A Book of Uncommon Prayer*

"At a time when male writers too often confine themselves to theology and apologetics, leaving spirituality to the women, Patrick Hannon has given us a thoroughly masculine, genuinely original, and refreshingly honest account of what it's like to be a twenty-first-century man of God. Yet this book will appeal to anyone, male or female, who is willing to do some serious wrestling with the soul."

Paula Huston
Author of *The Holy Way*

"A lively guide to living out faith in the everyday from an engaging storyteller who knows how to recognize those moments of grace that make our lives sacramental."

Judith Valente
Author of *Atchison Blue*

SACRAMENT

Personal Encounters
with Memories, Wounds,
Dreams, and Unruly Hearts

God Bless

Pat Hannon, cm

Patrick Hannon

ave maria press AmP notre dame, indiana

© 2014 by the United States Province of Priests and Brothers, Congregation of Holy Cross

Founded in 1865, Ave Maria Press is a ministry of the United States Province of Holy Cross.

www.avemariapress.com

Paperback: ISBN-13 978-1-59471-544-0

E-book: ISBN-13 978-1-59471-545-7

Cover image © gettyimages

Cover and text design by David Scholtes.

Printed and bound in the United States of America.

Library of Congress Cataloging-in-Publication Data

Hannon, Patrick, 1959-

  Sacrament : personal encounters with memories, wounds, dreams, and unruly hearts / Patrick Hannon, C.S.C.

    pages cm

  Includes bibliographical references.

  ISBN 978-1-59471-544-0 (pbk.) -- ISBN 978-1-59471-545-7 (ebook)

  1. Sacraments--Catholic Church. 2. Catholics--Anecdotes. I. Title.

  BX2200.H285 2014

  264'.0208--dc23

                              2014012301

To Michael McGregor,

for getting me to see that dark places aren't so scary after all.

Contents

Acknowledgments

I would like to acknowledge any number of essayists and writers whose bravery, honesty, and deft ability at crafting sinewy and startling sentences encouraged me to go deeper into my own thinking, particularly Brian Doyle, Annie Dillard, Flannery O'Connor, George Orwell, and James Baldwin.

Introduction
In a Field of Tall Grass

I am not sure if I can establish a direct correlation between the two events, but about the time that my second-grade teacher, Sister Anna Maria, told my classmates and me the story about how a bull once charged her father—by her account the most famous matador in all of Spain—and, with one flick of the bull's horns, launched him into the air and completely out of the stadium, where he landed on his feet unscathed, I began to think that maybe I could be a superhero, not unlike Superman. At my insistence, my mother one day sewed a beach towel onto a tee shirt of mine on which I had already painted an *S* with a colored marker. So you might imagine how amazingly fantastic I looked that Saturday morning, when I put on my superhero outfit and ran into the street, confident that no one would recognize me—as was the case with the real Superman—without my thick glasses on.

What prompted Sister Anna Maria to tell us that story about her father the bullfighter, I'll never know, but she was at the time preparing us for our First Holy Communion, and she was, in fact, telling us all sorts of impossible stories that captivated us and kept us cooing and well behaved. A virgin from a Podunk Palestinian town gave birth to the Son of God, the boy King. Choirs of angels serenaded shepherds, and Magi from the east came bearing gifts. Sister told us things about Jesus that we second graders could scarcely imagine but tried to anyway: He walked on water, she told us. You don't say. He fed thousands with a few loaves of bread and a couple fish. Love it. One day, she told us, Jesus extracted a legion of demons from one tortured, banished soul who lived alone among the tombs (you can imagine how much we all loved *that* story—including Sister) and cast them all in a flock of swine that then proceeded to stampede off a cliff—much to the amazement of the crowd and to the horror of the swineherd. She told us about the Last Supper, of course, and what followed—a sad story we knew by the somber tone of Sister's voice in its retelling: his numbing anguish in the dark garden; the betrayal and denials and desertion of all his friends and family save a loyal few, his suffering and death on a cross, his words of mercy piercing the thick darkness forever. I remember walking the three miles home from school around that time and seeing, I thought, in a field of tall grass near the fire station, Jesus looking at me. I thought I saw him once in the meat section of Romley's Market, across the street from the fire station. And once more peeking from behind a tree near the school's incinerator. Everywhere I turned, it seemed, I was seeing Jesus, as I imagined him, smiling, relieved.

I can't speak for my classmates, but Sister had me eating out of her hand with those stories of Jesus. She put me there in the boat on the raucous sea, in the hungry crowd on that high plain at dusk. She had me hiding in the graveyard that day near Gennesaret, too afraid of that man in chains to venture out. She had me in the upper room on that Holy Thursday and later in the garden and then on Golgotha. I was there at the foot of the Cross looking up as Jesus looked down. At me. And of course I was there at his tomb—got there earlier than anyone else—to see those brawny, giggling angels pushing the huge stone away from its entrance as if it had been made of Styrofoam, to see Jesus walking out, smiling, stretching his arms as one who had awakened from a long, deep slumber, his face magnificent and refreshed in the dawning light. I think now it must have been in second grade, while I sat enraptured by a great storyteller with a heavy Barcelonan accent, that I consciously began to believe in Jesus Christ and began to believe that it was possible to do great things, impossible things, noble and generous and courageous things, and that on my way to imagining myself as Christlike, I could, intermediately, see myself as Superman.

Perhaps this is how the gift of faith is effectively given to us human beings: first comes our ability, and our willingness, to imagine—to see with a painter's eye, to hear with a poet's ear, to smell and taste with an epicurean nose and palate, to touch with the fingers of a clay potter the created world—and to so be moved by the encounter that we can, in an instant, actually experience ourselves slipping into a dimension we never before knew existed, where time and space evaporate into an eternal now and here, where, in what we might call a mystical moment—think, for instance, of a stroll at sunset, the cradling of a newborn, a lover's kiss, the letting go of a grudge, or, dare we dream, a Chicago Cub's World Series championship—in that eternal here and now, the impossible becomes possible, the lines of division become porous and unsustainable, and we become, perhaps for only an instant, the people we always hoped we could be.

In *that* soil of undying, heart-thumping hope, I think, the seed of faith is planted. Perhaps this explains the encounter Mary had with the angel Gabriel at the annunciation. Mary's first reaction to the angel's request was a skeptical one. ("How can this be?" the virgin girl said. Today, she might have said, "Say *what*?") She could, though, with a little divine prompting, imagine for herself that, as highly improbable a virgin birth was, nothing was impossible for God. She could, in her own flexible mind and heart, see it happening. And so she said yes. Thus was established, at least in Matthew and Luke, at the outset, a leitmotif that will recur over and over in all the gospel accounts: Jesus confronting a skeptical, sometimes jaundiced world, a people too tired, too defeated, too cynical, too blind or unfocused or distracted to believe that the impossible was possible. Jesus, in short, came to teach us adults how to imagine once again and to see, in this opening wide of the senses of our souls, the beginning of our salvation.

This might help to explain why Jesus told so many stories (and why I love hearing them over and over) and why he said that, so far as he was concerned, the only way any of us adults can ever hope to enter the reign of God is to somehow reclaim our childlike wonder and awe at life—that is, our ability to imagine.

Because isn't it true that every day each of us wakes up to a story that we have titled "My Life" and that, beginning with our birth (or—why not?—our conception), each of our lives has been marked by a narrative arc extending from here to eternity, and that, on our good days, enjoys a seemingly infinite number of plot twists, and is filled with fascinating characters and settings, conflicts and resolutions, tensions and a denouements, which will in the end (as St. Paul wrote to the church of Corinth), dazzle us to no end and leave us breathless?

Every day, we awake to a world of possibility, armed only with our wits, imagination, and faith that remind us, when we most need to be reminded, that what was begun in us so long ago will be brought to completion. Surely this is a happy ending if there ever was one. These holy weapons in the hands of believers can defeat the deepest darkness and steel our spines for those moments when we embark on that daunting journey into the depths of our soul (a place D. H. Lawrence called "the deep vast forest") where the Deceiver comes stalking and tries to sell us the Great Lie: that we have no future, that hope is childish, and that we are alone. With faith and imagination, we become resilient instruments of hope in the hand of God. This makes me think of a conversation a priest friend of mine had with a young woman once. "Father," she said, "You know what kind of woman I want to be?"

"Tell me," he said.

"I want," she said, "to be the kind of woman who, when she gets up out of bed in the morning and her feet hit the ground, she hears the devil say, 'O, crap, she's up.'"

Imagine a bullfighter being tossed out of an arena by a bull's charge and the flick of his horns, and imagine him landing on his feet safe and sound. I suppose, in our universe, tethered to our particular laws of physics, this imagining is nothing more than fanciful and entertaining, a campfire tale. But imagine another universe in the multiverse (which, in fact, many theoretical physicists are doing—imaginatively—this very moment) where the laws of physics are more accommodating, and there you have it.

I remember coming home from school that day in second grade and telling my older brothers about that story, and they got a good laugh out of it, which angered me because they seemed to be implying that Sister Anna Maria wasn't telling the truth. Perhaps her story unwittingly served the Truth in a different way; perhaps the story's purpose was intentionally hidden from me back then and was, in its own way, a shovel turning and loosening the soil of my imagination. Maybe Sister Anna Maria was giving me permission—the way the angel did for Mary—to believe that nothing is impossible with God. And to see now the crucial role the human imagination plays in the calculus of faith. Without it, faith becomes staid, predictable, and safe. With it, faith becomes muscular, defiant, surprising.

I'm reminded now of a seventeen-year-old Chicago boy I knew years ago whose faith, I was to discover, was sinewy and taut. One day, in a small Irish village, he gave a baseball cap—his treasured, smelly, tattered Notre Dame baseball cap—to a wee Irish lad who had a scar on his face, the remnant of a swipe his drunk father had taken at him years before with a box cutter. The older boy could have more easily given up his left lung, I suspect, but somehow it became evident—tangibly and hauntingly—that what was being asked of him was something more important than a lung. Somewhere deep inside him, he must have heard a voice telling him, *Love that little boy the best way you know how.* He hemmed and hawed interiorly. His brow furrowed at the thought. And then, on a grey morning, he placed his baseball cap on the boy's head—a boy who had been coveting that cap for ten straight days—shook his hand, and left. I watched this all from my rearview mirror. It was a little death—a letting go—playing out under the klieg lights of hope. Even now, still, I hear angels sing.

At this moment, the Cubs are playing the Houston Astros at Wrigley Field. Both teams are in the cellars of their respective divisions. I imagine that Chicago kid I knew is there. He'd be about thirty years old now. Perhaps he's married and has a few kids of his own by now. I see him rooting for his beloved Cubs in the way Cub fans do—that is, with a resilient and bruised heart. Whether he's bought a replacement cap I don't know. But what I believe is this: every so often, that fellow thinks of that Irish boy with a scar on his face wearing his baseball cap. And somewhere in Ireland, I hope, is that grown-up boy who has that cap still and who every so often thinks of that American kid who did what he thought was impossible: that one day he reached across a great divide and touched a scar, healing a deeper wound. Every so often I imagine they are thinking of each other at exactly the same moment. And that moment must surely be what heaven is like.

•

I'm thinking about heaven more these days. I guess I shouldn't be surprised. I've turned fifty—an age those of us over fifty refer to as "the new thirty." But to the younger set, I've already crossed some unbridgeable river. I'm closer to one eternity—the one inaugurated by my death—than to the other one that ended with my birth. So time, for me, as the Steve Miller song goes, "keeps on slippin', slippin', slippin' into the future." And I am mostly trying to hold on. Perhaps this explains my interest these days in Einstein's special theory of relativity that proves, among other things, that time is, in fact, flexible. I want to slow time down and *sacar el jugo* ("to squeeze the juice" as they say in Mexico) out of life. I want to slip, slip, slip into the *now*, the place that exists somewhere between my cells and soul, a kind of Neverland, where I depart from every morning and return to every night. I am, always, the boy in a man's body.

I'll admit it: I'm not one of those who pine for heaven. I am—sadly or happily, it really depends on the day—tethered to life on earth. For sure, some days I anticipate the moment when I see God face-to-face with the excitement my mother had once when we were driving home from Mass. Having gotten her terminal cancer diagnosis a few months before, she knew her days on earth were numbered. Her impending death didn't seem to bother her, though, and this intrigued me more than it distressed me. (How can you *not* be afraid of dying, I sometimes said to her silently. I was twenty-six years old at the time and still petrified of my own demise.) "Sometimes," she told me as she gripped the steering wheel with her tiny hands and then loosened them, "I think, I get to see your father and my mom and dad and Baby James and . . ." She stopped talking and I looked over; she seemed to be looking not *at* something far away but deep *into* something. "I . . . I . . . sometimes, I can't wait to get to heaven," she said.

I want *that* kind of faith, the kind that replaces sorrow with hope. The kind that loosens the tight grip we too often have on life. The kind that believes in something more sustaining than oxygen and earth. I suppose I do have a bit of that faith, but it always seems fragile and flighty to me. I seem to need to hold onto something tangible. So I often console myself with the words that Jesus once said to his disciples, about how a little faith ("the size of a mustard seed," he proffered) can do impossible things. With a little faith, I can believe that my life now is a lovely thing—good work and good friends, a health plan and a warm bed, a fierce tribe of a family and shared memories, books and films and Oregon wine and Irish ballads—an embarrassment of riches. But I can also—with a smidgen of faith—believe that something better awaits. "Eye has not seen, and ear has not heard, and has not entered the human heart, what God has prepared for those who love him," St. Paul wrote to the Corinthians, paraphrasing the poet-prophet Isaiah. The Isaiah text said at the end, "for those who *wait for* him." There's the rub. Love (and thus faith, necessarily) demands patience and trust, two virtues I often find myself in short supply of as I grow older. But I know I *want* to trust God. I want to loosen my grip and let go. And I know that this desire—a gift from God as valuable as faith, I think—suffices for now. Perhaps this holy desire—the soul panging for God—is what makes us most human.

On warm October days such as today I sometimes look down from my third-floor office window and see students tossing a Frisbee around or playing bocce ball in the late afternoon. The mild and soft sunlight casts them always in a most favorable light. And I'll admit, I can become wistful, even nostalgic, in those moments. Mostly, though, I enjoy watching them enjoying their youth. I'm thinking now of Walt Whitman's poem "Youth, Day, Old Age and Night":

> Youth, large, lusty, loving—youth full of grace, force,
>   fascination,
> Do you know that Old Age may come after you with equal
>   grace, force, fascination?
> Day full-blown and splendid-day of the immense sun,
>   action, ambition, laughter,
> The Night follows close with millions of suns, and sleep and
>   restoring darkness.

Whitman got it right. The line that seemingly separates young from old, day from night, is an illusion. A line, after all, has no width.

In the night, I do not dream of being young. In my dreams I'm always young. I fly and breathe underwater in my dreams. In my dreams I take in the world with the visual acuity of a tomcat, the ears of a greater wax moth (who, after all, has to contend with a bat's finely tuned echolocation tracking device), and a bloodhound's nose. I leap as does a child in my dreams and touch things with a spider's nimble, delicate tarsal claw. Old Satan, I think now, wouldn't stand a chance on this planet if we approached our waking hours with the same childlike verve and imagination that we so easily employ when we are asleep. *O, crap, she's up,* indeed.

Isn't this what the Christian doctrine of the Incarnation—and from this the Catholic understanding of sacraments—wants us to do? Namely, to look more carefully at this world of ours and see treasures buried in plain sight. To place our hands to the earth and feel its thumping, living pulse. To listen for God's voice in the rustling breeze, the child's sob, the cheering throng, the lapping wave. To taste God on wet lips, in a sip of Oregon Pinot Noir, and in salty air. And to smell the aroma of God in a nose-pressed baguette. God in the flesh and bone and blood, telling us, showing us, that he has never left us. Sacraments point us toward these bridges that span the infinite divide between heaven and earth, these swinging bridges on which angels skip with news too important for our human happiness to be kept secret: God is with us.

•

Sacraments are stories that pinch the human mind awake. What was it the Catholic writer Annie Dillard said about us when we go to Mass? We shouldn't be wearing those soft, frilly hats. No fedoras at Eucharist. "We should all be wearing crash helmets," she said. "Ushers should issue life preservers and signal flares; they should lash us to our pews. For the sleeping god may wake someday and take offense, or the waking god may draw us out to where we can never return." Part of me cowers at the thought. I wish not to awaken an angry God or give him any reason to think that I'm up for anything remotely dangerous. I recoil at discomfort generally and rather like my wide-screen television.

But part of me wants to be taken to a place from which I can never return. This impulse—which has to be holy, because it's both thrilling and terrifying to consider—must be evidence of the Holy Spirit at work in the world, this holy fire, lit under our behinds that gets us up and moving again—a flame that flickers the darkness away. Faith means going to dark, unfamiliar places—in our minds and hearts, for sure, but also in our souls. And nothing, it seems to me, can be more fraught with danger than that adventure. It's a high-wire act without a safety net. It's God's call of Abram who would become Abraham: *Lech-lecha!* Get up and go! *Where?* we might ask. Don't ask. Just go. And so the story of our faith began, not with Adam and Eve, but with Abram, who would become Abraham, who on one ordinary day heard the Lord say to him, essentially, don't worry about anything. Just get up and go with me on a journey, a journey into the lovely dark where sometimes even God seems to disappear. What a wild ride this is for us. The only one we can hold onto is the very one who is telling us to let go.

Another memory of my second-grade teacher, Sister Anna Maria, comes to mind now. It is afternoon recess, and Sister has commandeered one of the bikes from the bike rack. She is, to the squealing delight of her young charges, riding it all over the playground, darting in and out of kickball and softball games, her long, black woolen habit blowing in the wind. Several of the older sisters, their hands tucked primly within the outer folds of their habits, appear unamused. I am dumbfounded. I am seeing something wholly unexpected bordering on the preposterous. I am seeing, though I couldn't have put it in these words, an untethered soul. I had no idea how the story unfolding that afternoon on the playground was going to end. But I was riveted by the danger of it all. I still am.

1. Baptism

When it's sin versus grace, grace wins hands down. All sin can do is threaten us with death, and that's the end of it. Grace, because God is putting everything together again through the Messiah, invites us into life—a life that goes on and on and on, world without end.

So what do we do? Keep on sinning so God can keep on forgiving? I should hope not! If we've left the country where sin is sovereign, how can we still live in our old house there? Or didn't you realize we packed up and left there for good? That is what happened in baptism. When we went under the water, we left the old country of sin behind; when we came up out of the water, we entered into the new country of grace—a new life in a new land!

That's what baptism into the life of Jesus means. When we are lowered into the water, it is like the burial of Jesus; when we are raised up out of the water, it is like the resurrection of Jesus. Each of us is raised into a light-filled world by our Father so that we can see where we're going in our new grace-sovereign country.

Could it be any clearer? Our old way of life was nailed to the cross with Christ, a decisive end to that sin-miserable life—no longer at sin's every beck and call! What we believe is this: If we get included in Christ's sin-conquering death, we also get included in his life-saving resurrection. We know that when Jesus was raised from the dead it was a signal of the end of death-as-the-end. Never again will death have the last word. When Jesus died, he took sin down with him, but alive he brings God down to us. From now on, think of it this way: Sin speaks a dead language that means nothing to you; God speaks your mother tongue, and you hang on every word. You are dead to sin and alive to God. That's what Jesus did.

Romans 5:21–6:11

Open Wounds

Until relatively recently—say, within the last ten years—it always struck me as odd, and a little unsettling, that when the resurrected Jesus appeared to his disciples, he still bore the wounds of the cross. Death had not defeated him, and yet his wounds remained, gaping and exposed. This never made sense to me. Had *I* been in charge, I would have made sure those wounds had healed. The encounter Thomas (and others, I suppose) had with the wounds of Christ, then, must have been catechetically instructive to the early followers of Jesus and the early Church, and must be for all of us baptized Christians now. By Jesus' wounds we were (and still are) healed. There's no way around those wounds. They seem to want to say something crucial about who we are as human beings and about the redemptive power of the risen, wounded Christ. The sacrament of Baptism—in the days of our ancestors we adults would have taken off all of our clothes and let the priest submerge us into the water—becomes a visible act of surrender, of capitulation to God's complete self-gift of love. Baptism is a sacrament of Christ's wounds that heal, and of the joy and freedom and hope they promise. It is the shadow of the Cross touching the edge of the empty tomb. It is letting go of our old, tired, self-absorbed, anxious, wounded selves and claiming a new identity in Christ, one no longer beholden to fear, shame, and regret. With baptism, we join the Church—a ragtag, astonished, and grateful band of wounded believers—who no longer sees our wounds as something to hide.

•

Around fifteen years ago I saw, for the first time, a man without a nose. Where his nose should have been was a gaping, triangular cavity, a smooth opening to a tiny cave. He was drinking a beer alone at the far end of a dank Portland bar. He wore his thinning gray hair in a neat ponytail that fell to his shoulder blades. His long shirt sleeves were rolled up, exposing a tattoo on his drinking arm. The bartender stood cross-armed at the other end, watching a game on the television bolted to the far wall. From across the bar I pretended to look at a point between them, but I couldn't help stealing looks at the man's hole. What an awful thing, I thought, to lose your nose. Without a prosthetic, he appeared reptilian.

Perhaps this explains in part why a few years ago that Taliban husband pinned his fleeing eighteen-year-old Afghani wife down and cut off her nose and ears. He hoped, I suspect, that he could rob her of her humanity. More than any other appendage, the nose seems to make us recognizably human. The ancients understood the symbolic power of the nose. That virtually every Egyptian statue in antiquity is missing its nose, for instance, is no coincidence. Marauding armies chiseled off those noses to send a message to the defeated: your gods can't save you. What divine power those statues exuded was cut off at the nose.

At the time of my encounter with the nose-less man, I was a young Catholic priest working in parish a few blocks away. The idle and addled parked their bikes and shopping carts in our church lobby, drank our strong coffee, and ate our day-old donuts. Many slumbered rainy mornings away curled up in the dry pews of the church, their arms tucked snugly between their legs. At the moment of consecration at the daily noon Mass, the Sanctus bells would jingle and the groggy would hoist their aching heads; watch me lift the host, then the chalice; and then fall back asleep. One time a Native American fellow the size of a refrigerator interrupted me while I was preaching. He stumbled to the steps of the sanctuary, fell to his knees, stretched his arms out, and yelled, "Father, am I going to hell?" I stopped Mass, went to him, leaned down, and whispered that no, he was not going to hell. He thanked me and returned to his pew.

In other words, back then I lived with, around, and beside wildly broken people, this loose confederacy of stragglers: a few armless, a couple legless, and others booze-pickled and brain-muddled, an unanchored throng of mostly loveable misfits, all of their bodies in one way or another saying, "Look at me. Please." They knew, the way a wounded child knows subconsciously, that if they could get you to look at them for a few seconds, you would have to help them. You couldn't look at someone suffering and just walk away. Or if you could, then there must be something wrong with you.

I'm beginning to think there *was* something wrong with me back then. You can, I think, walk away without actually walking away. While sitting in the bar that afternoon, I couldn't see beyond that man's hole. He seemed a nice enough fellow. At one point I stood beside him and ordered another beer. I nodded at him. He nodded back and took a swig. I peeked at him. I was disturbed by his hole in a way I had never been disturbed before. It tugged at me, dared me not to look away. Later, the man looked into the mirror behind the bar and caught me staring.

Thinking of that man without a nose now, I wonder: would it have hurt if, while standing next to him for that brief moment, I had said something such as, "Excuse me, I noticed you don't have a nose. Can I ask what happened?" Why didn't I? Why didn't I introduce myself, ask his name, and buy him another beer? I don't think he would have minded. But then again, he might have. He might have told me to mind my own business and get out of his face. But I'll never know. I finished my beer, paid my tab, and left the bar.

Cancer. Cocaine. A knife fight. A bullet. A botched operation. A dog bite. I'll never know how the man lost his nose. Or how he felt about losing his nose. Or if he actually had a prosthetic but took it off because it chafed and, besides, he was in the company of people who knew him and loved him. I'll never know if he was a famous poet or a retired longshoreman. A convict or a saint. Or all of the above. I'll never know his story. Instead, I did the math: I put two and two together—gray ponytail plus tattoo plus near-empty bar plus hole in the middle of a face equals damaged goods—and steered clear of the man. There I was, a young priest *trained* to embrace such encounters ("Christ in distressing disguise," Mother

Teresa of Calcutta put it once) with soft eyes that could bridge distances, which said, in so many words, *Your wound does not frighten me*. Instead I left the bar feeling every bit the coward.

I recall now an encounter I had as a five- or six-year-old boy while at my town's swimming pool. A man without a leg sat on the edge of the deep end of the pool that hot summer afternoon and splashed his body with cool, chlorinated water. While he stirred the water with his good leg, his stump of cinched flesh which extended three or four inches from his swimming trunks, sat idle on the pool's concrete lip. I swam over and waded a few feet away.

"Can I touch your leg?" I said, pointing at his stump.

"No," he said, in a tone that seemed to suggest he might let me later. I said okay and swam away. Where was that boy when I needed him years later at that bar? This was not a rude or impolite boy but the boy who thought that a fleshy stump, far from being horrifying, pitiful, or sad, was yet one more fascinating encounter in a world brimming with intrigue, that boy for whom a stump was touch-worthy. I fear that boy sized me up a long time ago—noticed, sadly, how risk-averse I had become to broken people, how I steered clear of alluringly dark places instead of running toward them as I once had—grew weary of me and of my duplicity, decided he had had enough, packed up, and moved away. I'm not sure exactly what I did when I got home to the rectory later that night. I probably ate dinner, prayed for the man without a nose and for all the broken people I had seen that day, and went to bed, ready to meet them again the next day on my terms. I had gotten used to them without having to actually join their ranks. I thought I loved them, but how can you really love someone unless you're willing to bleed with him?

•

Perhaps it was karmic payback that a year or so after my encounter (or my un-encounter) with that man with a hole in his face, I looked into the mirror and saw that some disease had struck my forehead overnight, along with the edges of my nostrils and my upper cheeks, leaving them bumpy, reddened, scabbed, and painfully dry. I had no idea what was going on. It seems oddly hysterical to say it now, but I thought I was dying. I stared at myself in the mirror again and recoiled at my reflection. I looked hideous, leprous. Walking to work that day—I was now a Catholic high school English teacher on the edge of Chicago's Northside—I wouldn't have minded being invisible. I didn't want anyone to see how ugly I had become and how ugly I felt.

During the first few days of my affliction no one said anything. Maybe my ailment wasn't so bad, I thought. When no one was looking, I picked at the sores, hoping they would disappear. I scrubbed the infected patches with industrial-strength soap twice a day, coated my face with Noxzema skin lotion every night, and prayed that when I awoke I would be healed. But every morning, before lifting my body out of bed, I fingered my face gingerly for the telltale bumps and found them.

I could tell instantly when one of my students noticed my off-putting skin disease; when a colleague took his eyes off mine for a millisecond and glanced at my blotchy forehead; or when a parent scanned my nose, my cheeks, or the patch of infected skin below my left eye. I knew what they were thinking: *This fellow is unclean.* One day a freshman boy looked at me queerly, but not unkindly, and said, "What's going on with your skin?" I still had no idea, so I said something lame such as, "Oh, it's just a little skin irritation." A few minutes later I locked myself in the nearest bathroom, stared once more into the mirror, and nearly cried.

I began skipping dinners with my brother priests. I breakfasted alone and lunched in my office. My attitude toward overhead fluorescent lighting, which cast me—at least to myself—as a meth addict, turned despondent. I combed my hair down instead of over and kept my head down. I saw clean—milky-white or tanned—unblemished skin as a private country club to which I had once belonged.

My face continued to deteriorate in public. Even the most forgiving light now mocked me. So, when I wasn't in the classroom, I sat alone in dimly lit rooms. I think it was then that I began to appreciate the insidious ability of a wound to isolate a human being and how these moments of self-imposed exile help to explain why a prosthetic arm, leg, hand, or nose serves more than a practical purpose. They get you out of the house and back walking and running in the world, for sure. But they also fill in deeper amputated spaces. I think they get us to see ourselves as we once were before the accident, illness, or violent act, before the phantom pain. Stepping out with or without a prosthetic device now seems to me a heroic act of defiance against our darkest voices. It announces a kind of inauguration, a new normal.

I was far from feeling normal back then, because my illness—and the hole it seemed to create inside me—couldn't be covered up prosthetically. Finally, I approached a friend for the number of his dermatologist. It embarrasses me now to think I had such little courage then, given that I had expended all of it in asking for a doctor's contact information. I made the appointment for later that day, drove to the clinic three towns away, filled out the paperwork, and said a prayer as I walked into the examining room. I expected to hear that I had stage-four melanoma. It took the doctor all of one unremarkable minute to diagnose my condition: rosacea, a lovely sounding (from the Latin "rose-colored") but incurable chronic skin ailment. He gave me prescriptions for an antibiotic and a topical ointment and told me to avoid using skin lotion on it anymore (as it turns out, skin lotion exacerbates the rosacea symptoms), use sun block on sunny days, drink wine and beer sparingly, and see him in a month. The rosacea blots began to recede a few days later, and I rejoined the semi-blemished world.

So I have an incurable disease. It's not going to kill me, but when I least expect it, my skin will turn seditious, go splotchy, and send me running for my topical ointment.

•

If you don't know this already, every time you see a new doctor, they make you own up to your past. They call it "your medical history," but really, it's an interminable, two-page, single-spaced journey into sickness and pathology that I bet leaves even the healthiest patient a little numb and nervous. Maybe it's just me at fifty-three, but checking those boxes (which I had to do recently) leaves me feeling awfully mortal. You know they have good reason to poke into your sometimes-embarrassing past, but it still feels a bit voyeuristic as they rummage around in places even *you* don't like to go. But you endure the trial—as you will later tolerate the skimpy gown they tell you to wear and the inevitable poking—with as much dignity as you can muster.

You don't know how many ways you can get sick and die until you fill out one of those questionnaires: "Have you ever had or have you now" followed by a list of diseases. High blood pressure, high cholesterol, a tumor, a growth, a cyst, cancer, gout, anemia, and so forth. When I filled out my medical history that afternoon at the dermatologist, I answered truthfully—except for one small lie. I didn't check the "yes" box that asked if I "had ever had or have now depression." I checked the "no" box on that one.

I don't suffer from depression. I like to call it "melancholy" because it sounds less clinical and more poetic, more Irish. I don't know if the category actually exists, but I am what I like to call "a functional melancholic." I live, and occasionally thrive, in a world of sneaking, creeping shadows. Thankfully, my chronic melancholy, like my rosacea, won't kill me. It will, I suspect, make me feel as if I'm living in a Van Gogh painting off and on for the rest of my life. I never know when the shadows will come, but when they do, I sigh heavily without anyone ever seeing it. I think about surrendering and then wait. The waiting is exhausting, by the way.

I'll be having a particularly good time with friends and then, for no reason, this gnawing sadness descends and I feel myself being pulled back into the darkness, as if that cold, empty place is my true home. I'll be saying Mass at the altar and all of a sudden I will not believe what I am doing and saying: I'll hear myself saying the words of consecration; I'll see myself lifting the host and the chalice; and a deeper voice will say, "You know you don't believe any of this." And then with the stink of fraud, I soldier on. Every now and then I fantasize about stopping the next time that happens and leaving the altar for good.

And then, as fast the sadness comes, it goes, and I believe again. I believe in God and heaven and angels and love and the basic decency of human beings. And I thank God that no one can see what I look like inside, how ugly my thoughts are sometimes and unattractive my soul. I thank God that I am one of the lucky ones who can pretend that I am not broken in some fatal way.

I've never been medically treated for my melancholy, though after my father died of a massive heart attack when I was twenty-five, I came close to going on Prozac. Instead, I decided to take time off from seminary classes and, with my spiritual director, tend to the matter of grieving my father's unexpected death. I sat one day in one of my professor's offices and informed him of my decision.

"What would your father want you to do?" the old priest—an Iwo Jima survivor—said bluntly. I imagined my father sitting next to me.

"He would want me to stay," I said.

"Then stay."

I stayed and completed the semester before everyone else.

So, apparently I was pretty tough. A classmate confirmed this a few weeks later as we walked around the lake one day. "I don't know how you do it," he said. I lapped it up, I have to tell you. I loved knowing that other people saw me as a strong person. It was who I always wanted to be and how I wanted to be seen. What I didn't tell him—how could I?—was that I went to bed most nights thinking it would be okay if I didn't wake up the next morning.

So I might be forgiven for not being completely truthful to my dermatologist about my past that afternoon a few years later. I had gotten used to appearing essentially unbroken. My apparent flaws were garden variety and easily forgivable: impatience, a bit of Irish temper, too loud a laugh, the occasional dirty joke, and a bit of laziness. I was so determined to bolster this self-narrative that by then I'd begun to see my hidden wound as a kind of gift. It made me more sensitive to another's suffering, I convinced myself. It made me a better priest. (Later, I would say it made me a better writer.)

People will wonder, I cautioned myself, how you can appear so happy all the time. So, if they ask, don't lie. Tell them that sometimes you're not happy. Tell them that it's not really about being happy anyway. Tell them it's about joy. Tell them that the seeds of joy are often planted in the soil of suffering, a pious thought that rings true as far as Christians (and lots of other people) are concerned. Don't tell them, though, that sometimes you entertain significant doubts about this rather crucial, life-altering truth that you've banked your whole life on. Don't tell them that your default stance toward the world is sadness. Give those who most desperately need it hope to hang onto. Imagine how powerful a lure this hope-textured thought was for me. I could subvert weakness, bend it to my will, and make it strong. I could pretend, in the end, that I was intact after all. I would tell people it was the crucified, wounded Christ living in me, but it was, I know now, Christ on the cheap. I would still keep my distance from his wounds and mine.

One night around the time of that doctor visit, I went with a friend to the Checkerboard Lounge on Chicago's Southside. The blues club was situated among acres of tired, cement-block public housing towers; boarded-up homes; empty, cyclone-gated plots; and dimly lit storefronts. We sat in a booth in the back, two white boys in a purple-lit room full of black bodies. Toward midnight, a sixtyish woman, mascaraed and pearled, made her way to the piano, stood at the microphone a few yards away, straightened her dress, and began to sing. She mesmerized me. Her dark chocolate skin glistened with a working woman's sweat. The Billie Holiday number she was singing slowly moved across the floor, reached down, down, down into me, further than I thought possible, and rummaged around as if searching for something important, maybe even precious. Having found nothing, the song withdrew, leaving me disoriented in the dark. When she finished, everyone applauded. She wiped her brow with a handkerchief and, with pursed lips, smiled sadly. At least that's how I saw it. She might have even smiled at me. It didn't matter. My friend and I stayed until she was done with her set and left. I walked to my car without saying a word. That's how my melancholy works.

•

Later that summer I took twelve of my Notre Dame High School boys to Ireland, an island that seems to me now a kind of Island of Blues. We spent a week with some Irish twelve- and thirteen-year-old kids who lived in a sad slice of Dublin not unlike the neighborhood that surrounded the Checkerboard Lounge, children who had, by their good behavior, earned a week's vacation on the Wexford coast, hiking, mountain climbing, kayaking, and swimming. These were tough Irish kids for whom everything was "fecking this" and "fecking that."

One of the Irish boys, I'll call him Brendan, had a scar that ran down his left cheek. Everyone knew that his father had cut him with a carpet cutter in a drunken rage a while back, so Brendan kept to himself mostly, rarely spoke, and never cried. The other boys occasionally gave Brendan the edge of their attention, and Brendan seemed fine with that. I instinctively drew back from this little boy's scar. I kept my eye on him, but from a safe distance.

One of the Chicago boys who had taken the trip, I'll call him Owen, came because his mother had told him he had to. A week before the trip, Owen's dad, a Chicago cop, had been arrested in a corruption sting and was sitting now in a Cook County jail cell. His mother thought the trip would do Owen good. A lanky seventeen-year-old with a mop of black hair, marble white and freckled skin, and a two-pack-a-day cigarette habit, Owen appeared fine.

One day early on, while everyone was getting ready to go kayaking, I saw Owen wrestling with a few of the Irish boys, tossing them into the sea, matching them cuss word for cuss word. He smiled and laughed heartily and honestly, which in retrospect makes me think that perhaps I might be right after all about those seeds of hope planted in sad soil, that maybe a little joy can be harvested even in dark days.

Everything about the Hook Peninsula that July morning said as much: the jagged granite cliffs and crags that hugged the coastline; the sun-sparkled, silvery-blue inlets and rivers and bays; the vast patchwork of tamed and tilled earth demarcated by crooked lines of stacked, uneven rocks; and the trees that jutted out defiantly from patches of barren earth, those bony trees the Irish poet Edna O'Brien suggested best described the Irish generally: "maimed, stark and misshapen, but ferociously tenacious."

And then, when he thought no one was looking, Owen's smile deserted him, his eyes darkened, and twenty years seemed to be added to his age. In that moment I saw Owen as he saw himself: essentially fatherless, untethered, and sinking fast without knowing why. *What will come of this boy?* I thought.

One night toward the end of the trip I went looking for Owen because he was not with us as we huddled around a bonfire on the beach. I found him a few blocks away, sitting with Brendan at the end of a pier. Owen's right arm cupped Brendan, held him close. I could hear Brendan sobbing.

•

I live in Portland now. It is autumn, my favorite season. I tell people, if they ask me why, a partial truth. I tell them I love the riot of reds and oranges and yellows of Portland's fall trees. I tell them I love the smell of fireplace smoke that blankets the street at sunset. What I don't tell them is that I love autumn mostly because it can't pretend. Autumn is a man without a nose. Autumn's a boy with a scar being held by a lost Chicago teenager who, I'm willing to bet now, was holding on for dear life himself. Oh, autumn puts on a good show for a brief moment, but in the end it knows it must surrender to a cold, distant sun. Everyone can see that autumn is all about self-exposure, about stripping down, turning everything inside out, and lying bare. Autumn is, it seems to me, about dying, about letting go, leaf by leaf. Perhaps I love autumn most because it is the most melancholic of seasons. It's the one season when I try hardest not to pretend that I'm in any way whole, or that I will ever be whole. In autumn I imagine living inside out, exposing the wounds I keep mostly hidden the rest of the year.

A few weeks ago I went back to that bar where I had first met that man without a nose. A tony bistro now occupies the site. I sat outside and drank a beer. I rubbed my forehead. My rosacea was hibernating, so I remained, thankfully, unnoticed. Watching men in suits and women in heels making their way down the street—to buses and cars on their way home—the sadness returned. It could have been anything. My sadness has a thousand triggers. It could have been the yellow-tipped tree across the street, a whiff of perfume, or the sound of a bike tire on asphalt.

Nonetheless, couples chatted and laughed as they sauntered by my table, oblivious to my particular darkness. They all looked happy to me. Bikers wove in and out of traffic. A streetcar stuffed with passengers sailed past me. I thought of what a priest once said to Freud, when Freud asked what he had learned after years of hearing confessions. "No one is as happy as they appear," the priest told Freud, and Freud thought that sounded about right. My own time hearing confessions, for what it's worth, tells me he was right, too. The thought that we're all walking wounded in one way or another comforts me. If I thought for a moment that happiness was an actual earthly destination, I would, I think, lose all hope, because I know I'll never reach that Shangri-La while I'm living.

I used to think I was one of the lucky ones because my wounds were easily concealed. I don't anymore. I know that I skate on thin ice, never knowing for sure if and when the ice is going to crack and give way.

I sat drinking my beer that late afternoon and thought of that man without his nose. I thought about how you only get to move forward in life. He went on with his life, and I went on with mine. Still, I thought about that time when our lines crossed, when for a brief moment our eyes met in that mirror, and how I probably missed out on a great story. I thought that maybe life is filled with all these little moments that pop in as fast as they pop out, these strange, human, particle-like encounters of unfathomable depth that can transport us in a heartbeat to places we can scarcely imagine going.

A chilly wind kicked up. I zipped my jacket up and thought I should probably go. I breathed deeply, took in the smells of autumn, and felt once again the hope that comes, at least to me, like sadness, unexpectedly. Perhaps autumn gives me the solace that faith cannot provide. Or maybe it's this way: autumn reminds me that faith is not about holding on; it's about letting go, about rushing into the darkness and not away from it. It's not about seeing but about fumbling in the dark. It's about not having to dress this inward journey with soft, lacy language, however well intentioned. Maybe it's enough to simply bare the scar, leave the nose at home, face the dull loneliness that comes with wounds of any kind, and get on with living. Maybe faith is skating like crazy on thin ice, hoping beyond hope that if the ice starts giving way, the cracks will appear behind you.

2. Confession

When they got to the place called Skull Hill, they crucified him, along with the criminals, one on his right, the other on his left.

Jesus prayed, "Father, forgive them; they don't know what they're doing."

Dividing up his clothes, they threw dice for them. The people stood there staring at Jesus, and the ringleaders made faces, taunting, "He saved others. Let's see him save himself! The Messiah of God—ha! The Chosen—ha!"

The soldiers also came up and poked fun at him, making a game of it. They toasted him with sour wine: "So you're King of the Jews! Save yourself!"

Printed over him was a sign: THIS IS THE KING OF THE JEWS.

One of the criminals hanging alongside cursed him: "Some Messiah you are! Save yourself! Save us!"

But the other one made him shut up: "Have you no fear of God? You're getting the same as him. We deserve this, but not him—he did nothing to deserve this."

Then he said, "Jesus, remember me when you enter your kingdom."

He said, "Don't worry, I will. Today you will join me in paradise."

Luke 23:33–43

Moon Rising

I have a brother who's not been to confession in years. Decades perhaps. He threatens to wait until his deathbed, where I, his younger brother and the priest of the family, will, presumably, be compelled to hear it at last. I wish he wouldn't wait so long between visits, but I can understand why. It's a daunting task to sit in a (usually) uncomfortable chair a few feet from a priest, who is sometimes hidden and sometimes not, and spill your guts. Those few minutes can be harrowing, but not for reasons my brother might think. He probably likens confession to a dental drilling, a necessary procedure best postponed. But as one who sits on both sides of the confessional box, I see the sacrament as a kind of strip act (cue the uncomfortable dream where we find ourselves at Burger King ordering a Whopper in our underwear). Neither of us—priest or penitent—*enjoys* exposing our bad acts, our dark thoughts, our grudges, and our secret failures. But for us Catholics, don't these moments of holy honesty, this stripping away of pretense and pomp, draw us closer to what being fully human is all about? Perhaps the loneliest among us are those who are walking through their lives with all their secrets intact.

•

As a boy I couldn't seem to hold a grudge for very long. My monthly Saturday-afternoon visits to the confessional saw to that. "You've been forgiven, so go and forgive," Father Stack would tell me in his soft Irish brogue every time before I slunk out of the box, as if he knew something about me that no one else did. Somewhere between Father Stack's absolution and my kneeling before the tabernacle to say my three Our Fathers and three Hail Marys, it seemed I had wiped everyone's slate clean, an act of mercy that always surprised me. Forgiving Tim Rogers once again for calling me a dick and punching me when Sister wasn't looking, for instance, always seemed to me, and still does, an unnatural act of unilateral surrender foisted upon me by a demanding and unreasonable God. On the other hand, a healthy grudge, fine-tuned by natural selection, I suspect, protects us—moat-like—from an unforgiving world. A furrowed brow sends an unambiguous message to any foe that the grudger's memory is prodigious and that he won't be small or vulnerable forever.

Boys at my Catholic school who got a reputation for forgiving bullies might have garnered admiration from the nuns and priests, but their peers dismissed them without pity. It was almost as if they were asking for it. So I knew, as I made my way from the church to recess, this forgiving business was not my doing. It had the Almighty's fingerprints all over it. Letting go of grudges, we were told, was a graceful act that drew its power from Christ nailed to the cross, and we would be wise to follow his example. But I could never seem to shake the feeling that somehow I would get the raw end of the deal if I did. So, if I forgave bullies back then, it was half-hearted. The other half kept a wary lookout, the half that knew I was essentially alone to fight my own battles. While I had four older brothers who, I suppose, would have intervened on my behalf if I had begged them back then, I also carried an Irish name and, with it, an aversion to begging of any kind. And to have another fight your battles burdened you with a shame greater than any humiliating defeat.

It seems providential then that when I was twelve, my Great-Auntie Ber told me the Kennedys were my cousins. She told me that Jack Kennedy took the oath of office on his maternal grandmother's—Mary Josephine Hannon's—bible and that Mary Josephine's father, Michael Hannon, came from a Limerick town named Lough Gur, which, as the crow flies, was less than three miles from Bruff, where my great-great-grandfather Patrick Hannon was born. For my birthday a few months before she died, she gave me an old history of Ireland, which I read cover to cover later that summer. I would come to appreciate that book as a helpful catechism and my reading of its stories, a sacred initiation rite. I suspect it was my Auntie Ber's intention all along to indoctrinate me early into a tribe from which I could draw, as from a well, courage to face my battles alone. Perhaps she saw me as Father Stack saw me (each working at cross-purposes, it seems to me now): a boy with a confederate memory, a heart easily bruised and loyal, and a temper in need of focus.

With little fuss I pivoted from my baseball heroes named Jackson, Rudy, Bando, and Campaneris to those Hibernians named

Boru, O'Connor, O'Neil, Parnell, O'Connell, and Collins. And just as quickly, I learned to despise Richard "Strongbow" de Clare, all the kings and queens of England since Richard II (especially Elizabeth I, William of Orange, and Victoria, "The Famine Queen"), and, most of all, Oliver Cromwell, before whose ugly, Puritan visage on the page—a soulless man with a soul patch below his lower lip—I would grimace and mutter "you bastard" and mean it.

The more I read my Irish history, the more implacable my grudge became: the slaughters, the hungers, the penal laws, and the daily humiliations spread lavishly over centuries of oppression and occupation. And, at least by the summer of 1972, the bully British had yet to apologize for any of their sins, let alone offer repentance or seek forgiveness. About that time I began staying up late to watch *Monty Python's Flying Circus*. The sketch comedy's stinging parody of English poshness, hypocrisy, arrogance, false humility, prudishness, and hypersensitivity to class fed my animus and thrilled me. My capacity to hold a grudge grew exponentially. Much to my surprise, I discovered I could nurture a rancor toward an entire people. Many of those skits I committed to memory. It was clear to me then that I was not laughing *with* the British. I was laughing *at* them.

Soon after Auntie Ber died, the Tunney family from Ulster's County Tyrone (where Owen Roe O'Neill led the Catholic rebels to a famous victory at the battle of Benburb in 1646) packed up their belongings, left their home five thousand miles away, and moved in next door. I became quick friends with Edmund, a boy my age, who taught me most of the rebel songs. We often sat together with his melancholic father on their porch on those first summer nights and, to Mr. Tunney's guitar strumming, sang them all. My favorite, the one we often saved for last, was "Four Green Fields," a wailing lament of Ireland, personified in the song as a long-suffering, ancient woman. The middle verse went:

> Long time ago, said the fine old woman
> Long time ago, this proud old woman did say

There was war and death, plundering and pillage
My children starved, by mountain, valley and sea
And their wailing cries, they shook the very heavens
My four green fields ran red with their blood, said she.

I recall one summer evening in particular after we had sung that song. Red-eyed and a bit tipsy, Mr. Tunney seemed troubled. He scratched the back of his head roughly, as if trying to shake something loose; he muttered under his breath in Irish. Edmund's wary eyes told me we'd be better off letting his father be. Finally, Mr. Tunney lifted his bulky frame from the stoop, sighed deeply, grabbed his guitar, and disappeared into the house without saying a word. Edmund and I sat together for a few minutes quietly, our shoulders touching. I could hear him breathing. We finally said good night and I walked home haunted by those wailing babies dying in their mothers' arms before fading peat fires. I wanted to hit someone. I thought of those British soldiers who had recently gunned down two dozen unarmed Irish Catholic protesters on bloody Derry Sunday, seven of the boys not much older than me. Perhaps Mr. Tunney's heart bled for those fallen boys that night. Perhaps he even knew some of them; any Tyrone town was no more than an hour from Derry, after all. My father was watching the news on the TV when I entered the house. Seeing me quickly wipe my eyes with my hands, he asked me what happened. "Nothing," I said, and I went to my room and lay on my bed in the dark, startled that I could feel pain and anger for people I never knew.

If you claim even a hint of British ancestry and find my confession alarming, allow me to stipulate that I did not dislike you *personally* then. I had no design on your or your relative's scalp specifically. I can't think of a single British person who has ever wronged me (though Tim Roger's surname strikes me as perniciously English). But the wounds inflicted on the Irish by the British over the span of eight hundred years began to appear strangely on my skin nonetheless. Only I alone could see them. In a short time I couldn't talk about who I was without in some way alluding, however tangentially or subtly, to my Irish roots and wounds. Irish ballads, poems, and legends delivered the Irish story soaked in sadness, quiet anger, revolt, and revenge—the poet Edna O'Brien's "maimed, stark, and misshapen tree" of a narrative—and became mine. (Full disclosure: I'm three-quarters Irish, one-quarter German.)

•

It's easy to see now why I held onto this wounded identity as long as I did. Grudges enshrined in memory—even an ancient one grafted onto one's psyche—seem to provide lasting succor, solace, and meaning to the wronged and the oppressed, at least they did for me when I was younger. I was bullied in those days. Realizing that my personal plight and ungainly anger could be understood and appreciated as part of a larger, nobler narrative gave me hope. It linked me, however loosely, to a band of brothers and sisters against whose hardened hearts spears and bullets bounced. In such a grudge-dependent state one scarcely can (or wants to) allow for the possibility of mercy ever anchoring a more compelling, self-defining story.

It also seems to me that, if you let them, grudges offer an atoning explanation for almost any personal flaw, addiction, habit, or moral weakness. Though my well-known (and sometimes destructive) temper as a child preceded my animosity toward the English, I began to secretly blame my temper indirectly on my British-afflicted Irishness, for instance. Perhaps this explains why we hold onto grudges for as long as we do, why some of us are willing to be buried with them, and why we can, seemingly willy-nilly, resent even those we do not know personally. "Now I have a great many enemies," the Chinese writer Lu Hsun wrote in an essay titled "Death" that he penned shortly before dying, "and what should my answer be if some modernized person asked me my views on this? After some thought I decided. Let them go on hating me. I shall not forgive a single one of them either." Why seek healing when an open wound—real or imagined—promises so much more? Stitch up a wound and it will all but disappear in time, leaving us to face alone all our personal flaws and failings. The grudging voice within, on the other hand, tells us it's not our fault. One voice becomes two and then three. Soon we are serenaded in an echo chamber of soothing resentments and rationalizations sufficient for a lifetime.

I gain no pleasure from admitting to holding grudges. It embarrasses me—a Catholic priest who says Mass on most days and every Sunday and who spends a sliver of each week hearing confessions—that I need to be reminded by my dead mother of the destructive and irrational nature of this peculiarly human emotion. "You shouldn't hate anyone but the devil," she would tell me when I came home sputtering and red-faced from school as a boy, having been teased and taunted by the likes of Tim Rogers. I know of the corrosive, toxic nature of a grudge and how, if you allow a grudge to fester and grow into a full-fledged hatred, it can rot a person from the inside. But I cannot deny the grudge's place in my heart, however unwelcome it is. If it were simply a matter of wishing, I would have gotten rid of my grudges a long time ago. If Merck, Bristol-Meyer Squibb, or Abbott Laboratories were to miraculously create a pill that could free me from my grudges, I would (I think) take it. As it is, I'm left to my own feeble devices to fend them off when I can.

The best I can do is to look at them as they pace and growl in their cage and not blink. I think it's only fair to admit that the journey from "shouldn't" to "will not"—as it pertains to holding a grudge—is often long and lonely. I'm trudging on a dusty road these days, crowded as it is with slump-shouldered, cart-pulling refugees of every sort, all of us at once strangely burdened and buoyed by our grudges, each of us isolated in our own particular angers.

You would think that by virtue of my priesthood and Christian faith I would have evolved further, been transformed by that redemptive grace Dietrich Bonhoeffer spoke of so eloquently. He described a costly grace borne of a Savior's act of pure, unfettered forgiveness that grabs hold of my human heart and pleads for my unconditional surrender. Bonhoeffer, a German Lutheran minister and theologian, was hanged in 1945 for his role in the assassination attempt of Adolph Hitler. Despite the unsanitary and severe prison conditions he endured, he befriended his Nazi guards, who helped preserve his papers and correspondence and allowed him to minister to other prisoners. I think he died grudgeless.

You would think in the light of that wooden Golgotha cross I would have become more loving and accepting of others by now, quicker to forgive, and less grudging. Sadly, this is not the case. I think I was more forgiving when I was younger. I've not given up on myself, or on God, in this matter of letting go, though. Most nights I go to bed hoping to wake up a new person. If I am in fact less forgiving now, I am, I think, more humble, and that's not a bad place to be. I read somewhere that Gandhi admitted it took him fifty years of hard work to eliminate all hatred from his heart. I find this confession comforting.

I am happy to report, though, that I no longer wish the British ill. I took a trip to Oxford ten years ago to visit a nephew ("and to make peace with the people who have oppressed my people for eight hundred years," I told my students before I left), and I got to know a large number of delightful, witty, self-deprecating, thoughtful, playful, generous, and compassionate Brits there. They ruined the grudge forever, so I let it go. I still, however, enjoy a vestigial distaste for bangers and mash, Manchester United, the East End cockney dialect, and the British royal family, though I've softened a bit toward the queen. It's hard to dislike an eighty-five-year-old lady.

*

Nonetheless, I hold onto my other grudges pettishly and, on my bad days, with Gollum-like attachment. In fact, as is often the case, as soon as I dispense with one grudge, I acquire another, sometimes two, which both exasperates and deflates me. They come and go in various shapes and sizes: the guy who cut me off on Greeley Avenue; the woman I stood behind at the quick check-out lane at Safeway with more items in her cart than the sign per-mitted; the inattentive waiter at a Portland bistro that will remain unnamed, who apparently and inexplicably pegged me for a cheap tipper and gave me lousy service; a teaching colleague who still won't give me the time of day; and the relative who never returns my voice mails because he only texts. Like a mosquito bite or a rash, they frustrate, irritate, and distract me. They compel me to scratch, but truthfully, doesn't the scratching feel pretty good for a while? In the end, though, they take over, and all the scratching in the world will not alleviate the suffering.

I want to think that my life is not a series of incurring insults and bruising encounters, and mostly I do. I like to think that I'm a recovering grudge-aholic who tries to make it through every day without holding a grudge. But then someone comes along and, by some careless act or thoughtless comment, taps into my vast reserve of hidden insecurities, and I silently stew. I'm reduced once again and, at least in my own head, play the wounded child. It's not an attractive sight. In the end, the grudge, far from emboldening my flagging spirits, actually cuts me off from my better self, the one who, on a different, sunnier day, is forgiving, even to an oaf.

Perhaps this is the cruel logic of grudges: they unwittingly diminish us even as our inflated sense of self demands that we hold onto them. An insult, a slight, a cruel prank, or a thoughtless barb all seek to unmask us, don't they? They toy with us, as a cat does with a panicky mouse, to get us to see that we are, when you think about it, pretty small in the grand scheme of things. None of us want to think this. So, unjustly tarred, we cling to retributive justice; we wait patiently for karma to kick in. But if we're not careful, the soft cement of our unforgiveness will thicken, and we will get stuck.

Here's a grudge I've packed in cotton: I stood outside Our Lady of Perpetual Help Catholic Church in Glenview, Illinois, one Sunday morning a few years ago, having said Mass and preached like a Southern Baptist—that is, as one on fire. At the time, I enjoyed a reputation as a pretty decent preacher, based on coffee-and-donuts feedback, so when on this particular Sunday a middle-aged woman walked out of the church quickly, as if she wanted to beat the fawning crowd, I prepared myself for a compliment.

"Tell me," she said, "you say Mass here often?" She was not smiling, which confused me.

"Yes," I said, "I usually say Mass here every other Sunday."

"Do they usually publish the schedule in the parish bulletin?" Another fan, I thought.

"Yes, I believe they do."

"Good," she said, and she began to walk away. After traveling a few yards, she turned around and said, "Now I'll know when *not* to come. Your homilies stink."

I've not gotten over that encounter completely. The grudge festers, as if somehow my personal happiness depends on others seeing me as a great preacher. My hunch is she has probably long forgotten me, but I have never forgotten her. How do you forget someone who essentially taped a dozen sticks of dynamite to the foundation of what you *thought* was your authentic self, lit the fuse, and walked away without even looking back? I suppose she thought she was doing me a favor. I don't think she intended to be cruel. But a grudge places pillows over such generous thoughts and presses down firmly.

•

When it comes to managing my grudges these days then, I often feel like Lucy in that now-famous *I Love Lucy* episode in which she and Ethel are tasked with wrapping individual chocolates coming down a candy factory conveyer belt. Initially Lucy finds the work quite easy, but inexplicably the conveyer belt picks up speed, leaving them frantic to keep up. (They were threatened with dismissal if they couldn't.) They begin corralling chocolates into piles on the counter in front of them and stuff a slew of them down their shirts and into their pockets. "I guess we're fighting a losing battle," Lucy says nervously. And sure enough, when the belt stops, Lucy and Ethel take all the unwrapped chocolate and hide them under their chef hats and stuff their mouths with them. The forewoman returns, blind to the ruse, sees the empty conveyer belt, and registers her delight. "Fine!" she says, "You're doing splendidly." And then, calling to the person controlling the belt somewhere off stage, she says, "Speeeeed it up a little!" Like that conveyer belt, time is skipping past me at a pretty alarming clip these days, and the grudges keep coming.

I don't think I'm alone in saying that letting go of our grudges might be the hardest thing for a human being to do. I'm sure it has something to do with our precious egos and how much we are invested in this sense of ourselves as the center of the universe.

I think it has something to do with how children interpret the optical illusion of the moon traveling in the night sky. When we are walking and looking at the moon, it appears to be following and staring down at us. Children believe this is true. It isn't of course. But it strains the eyes to capture the truth sometimes: to widen the aperture enough to see, from a point far above, yourself among thousands and thousands of tiny creatures; or from a point in the stratosphere, to locate yourself, an infinitesimally tiny dot, on a continent; or even further out, let's say from a point near the sun, to find the Earth at all. It seems to me grudges do the opposite. They keep us firmly rooted in our own heads with our eyes focused inward at our wounded selves ("selfyeast of spirit," as Gerard Manley Hopkins put it, "the dull dough sours"); we see ourselves as the alpha and the omega, the only universe that matters, and the ultimate reality.

Martin Luther called this phenomenon "the heart turned in upon itself," and that sounds about right to me. Because the

opposite of holding a grudge—to extend mercy to the undeserving—seems to reorient the heart to its proper, outwardly focused
position. For whatever reason (Augustine called it original sin) our
default position seems to be self-centered. Apparently we have to
learn to forgive every time we are injured—that is, to point our
hearts outward again. Whole religious traditions (whole *Star Trek*
episodes, for that matter) have been constructed to address this
seemingly impossible task of forgoing our grudges for good. And
while at least one recent scholar has noted that we have become
a *less* violent species over the past few hundred years, he has not
made the claim that we have become a more merciful species.[1] But
maybe we should accept his thesis for the baby step in the right
direction that it purports to be. Most of us keep our grudges sim-
mering quietly on the stove these days, rather than seeking redress
through the bullet, the sword, or the spear. We watch our grudges
carefully, lest they boil over.

Grudge-holding starts early, too. Two of my grandnieces,
three-year-olds Frannie and Betty, are identical twins. You stand
zero chance of distinguishing the two at this point, I promise. I
could tell after a while they had grown weary of my confusing one
for the other, or even worse, of my playing the rather favorable
odds and calling out one name hoping I got it right. Finally, when
seeing them together one day I simply said, "Which one is Betty?"
Without smiling, they both raised their hands and looked at me.
Call it what you will: a gentle jab, an unexpected expression of
toddler wit, or a playful trick. Maybe I'm too sensitive an uncle, but
I saw a little sadness in their eyes at my seeming lack of concern
for them individually, as distinguishable persons. I can't establish a causal link, but right about that time, Frannie decided she
would only wear pants, and Betty developed an instant devotion
to dresses. The one thing I've always loved about children their age
and a little older is how seemingly easy it is for them to forgive,
how quick they are to hug a hurt away. But a year has passed, and

I've still not seen a dress on Frannie or pants on Betty. I wonder if they're holding a grudge.

I try to put myself in Frannie and Betty's skin. On some level their twin identity must be a source of growing concern these days, even as Betty gladly shaved her head three months ago for Frannie, who had lost her hair to chemotherapy. They don't know it yet, but they were carved from the same fertilized egg. They spooned in the same womb for nine months, during which they quite possibly sucked each other's thumb. But they must know instinctively, even if we can't see it so easily, that they are separate persons with distinctive quirks, habits, dreams, fears, and hopes. It seems to me now that every grudge begins first as a kind of revolt, a shivering of the spirit that balks at the notion clearly suggested by someone else that we are not special creatures, important and vital in our own unique and utterly mysterious ways.

•

I see now that holding a grudge comes naturally to us humans (and, I'm told from those who have owned them, potbellied pigs). Cain nurtured a huge grudge against his brother Abel. He may have held a grudge against God, too. The story of grudges goes that far back and that deep, apparently. Mercy then is often relegated to the heroic and holy and deemed more divine than human. The merciful always seem to surprise us mortals, so ingrained in us is the calculus of retribution that we cannot seem to fathom mercy as a gift for the undeserving.

A milk-truck driver stepped into a one-room schoolhouse in Nickel Mine, Pennsylvania, on a fall day in 2006, and shot eleven Amish girls, killing five before killing himself. Network and cable klieg lamps lit the valley for a week as we all sat open-mouthed listening to Amish parents talk about forgiving the killer, Charles Roberts IV. I read later that Mr. Leroy Zook—whose wife, two daughters (one of whom was the teacher), two daughters-in-law, and two baby grandchildren got out unharmed but not unshaken—went up and shook the hand of Charles Roberts's father at a town gathering. "I think it's helping him to meet people, too, and see that there's no grudge," Leroy Zook said. And here I am, still holding onto a grudge against a woman who told me years ago that I was a lousy preacher. What a colossal waste of time.

I'm guessing those merciful Amish knew who they were. One man's brutal—seemingly unforgivable—act would not poison their deep well of memory. Those million memories, it seems to me, coalesce eventually for each of us into stories uniquely our own. We stitch these memories nimbly together into quilt-like narratives that satisfy that deepest of human longings: to know in the deepest recesses of our hearts that we matter, that we count, and that in a vast, dark, and cold universe we exist for a reason. For some of us, though, when that sense of self, imbedded in memory, is called into question by a snub, an insult, a rejection, a jilt, a betrayal, a punch to the nose, a sneer, a stab, a lie, an undressing, a humiliation, a theft, or a dismissal, we bear the wound as a secret badge of honor. The challenge, I suppose, is to do what I suspect those Amish did: use the strength of the wound to defeat the despair that lingers in its shadow with a kind of memory jujitsu. Otherwise, I think, we can get pinned by the wound. Perhaps this effort to "fight back the burden of grief that is laid on each one of us," as Mark Twain put it, bestows upon the grudge some legitimate, temporary purpose: it props us up under heavy assault for a while and gives us, however thinly, a sense of dignity. I suppose in this temporary holding on of a grudge, one might gain wisdom from wounded memories.

Sadly lost in this calculus of mercy, it seems to me, is any thought that a wounded memory can actually be healed. A grudge, in this sense, becomes a wide-open wound unto itself, and with black hole pull, can swallow us whole if we let it. Perhaps then an awkward truth lingers in the shadow of every grudge, however big or small, suggesting that we hold onto our grudges because our wounds have become an important (some would say essential) part of our personal stories. Our wounds are welts that never go away or deep burns that scar the skin forever. We can't imagine a self separate from the wounds. Far from simply holding in cold storage these stories of defeat, failure, assaults, and cruelties that we thaw out every now and then for the cautionary tale or the self-deprecating yarn, lasting grudges get to dictate, in large part, how we see ourselves.

•

A few years ago I was giving a talk on the subject of mercy in a church basement in Shepparton, a small farming community a hundred miles north of Melbourne, Australia. It was the last talk of a long day, and I was tired. I stood at a podium looking up from my notes and onto a dozen or so very pious-looking Aussie Catholics who had come out to hear me. They sat in their metal folding chairs scattered across the cavernous hall, still bundled in coats and scarves in the cold room, grasping their Styrofoam cups of coffee. They listened intently as I talked about the merciful power of the Cross. Being a Holy Cross priest (our order's motto: *Ave Crux, Spes Unica*—Hail to the Cross, Our Only Hope), I was expected, if not to wax eloquent on the theme, to offer words of hope to these old men and women, most of whom I reckon had descended from those unlucky Irish who had been plucked from their homes and prison cells centuries ago, shoved onto penal ships, and sent to the bottom of the world forever so they could no longer bother their English overlords and jailors.

At one point I brought out the old bromide about that peculiar amnesiac condition that happily afflicts the Irish whereby they forget everything but their grudges, and everyone chuckled knowingly. An old man, sitting in a far corner, his face so creased and rural brown it looked like the inside of a walnut shell, closed his eyes, crossed his arms, and pressed his chin to his chest. He appeared to nod off. My talk and the Q & A afterward went for about an hour, after which we sat around and enjoyed each other's accents, polished off the tray of cookies and the gallon of coffee, and said our goodbyes.

The old man in the corner approached me last. He pushed a chair next to mine and sat down. He told me his story. Came from Ireland. *Which part?* The North. *Lovely.* Farmed in Shepparton fifty years. Wheat mostly. Raised five boys. *I have five brothers.* Lovely. One of my boys. He was with his friends on a boat outing to Tasmania. Port Arthur. Back in 1996. Used to be an old penal colony. *Didn't know that.* Now you do. A fellow came with a gun and bullets and shot and killed thirty-five people that day. Including my son. Wounded dozens more. *I'm sorry.* Thanks, Father. I've forgiven that man. You know why? *Why?* Because Jesus told me to. Forgive us our trespasses as we forgive those who trespass against us. I hold no ill will. I can't. Jesus told me to forgive, so I forgave the man.

Jesus, I thought. For some strange reason I believed the man. I took him at his word. I wanted to believe it was possible.

The old man lifted his lanky frame from the chair. I stood up. He shook my hand and said thank you. No, I said. Thank *you.* He walked across the long hall—his gait steady—opened the door and disappeared into the night. I sat down. Somewhere someone hit a switch and the basement hall went black. I stood and went to a window. I pushed the drapes away and looked out. Directly in front of me, across the road, hanging low above a far field, I saw the full, yellow moon flitting in and out of clouds. The moon seemed to be staring at me. As if I were the only one left on the planet.

3. Eucharist

L et me go over with you again exactly what goes on in the Lord's Supper and why it is so centrally important. I received my instructions from the Master himself and passed them on to you. The Master, Jesus, on the night of his betrayal, took bread. Having given thanks, he broke it and said, "This is my body, broken for you. Do this to remember me."

After supper, he did the same thing with the cup: "This cup is my blood, my new covenant with you. Each time you drink this cup, remember me."

What you must solemnly realize is that every time you eat this bread and every time you drink this cup, you reenact in your words and actions the death of the Master. You will be drawn back to this meal again and again until the Master returns. You must never let familiarity breed contempt.

Anyone who eats the bread or drinks the cup of the Master irreverently is like part of the crowd that jeered and spit on him at his death. Is that the kind of "remembrance" you want to be part of? Examine your motives, test your heart, come to this meal in holy awe.

If you give no thought (or worse, don't care) about the broken body of the Master when you eat and drink, you're running the risk of serious consequences. That's why so many of you even now are listless and sick, and others have gone to an early grave. If we get this straight now, we won't have to be straightened out later on. Better to be confronted by the Master now than to face a fiery confrontation later.

So, my friends, when you come together to the Lord's Table, be reverent and courteous with one another. If you're so hungry that you can't wait to be served, go home and get a sandwich. But by no means risk turning this Meal into an eating and drinking binge or a family squabble. It is a spiritual meal—a love feast.

1 Corinthians 11:23–33

Next Year in Jerusalem

A Holy Cross priest at Notre Dame I never really knew—Father Griffin—wrote a regular column for the school newspaper that he titled "Letters to a Lonely God." As a seminarian in the 1980s, I read him regularly. I think it was the thinly veiled melancholy that ran through his stories that struck the deepest chord inside me. My father had died suddenly from a heart attack in my first year of studies, and by the time I finished three years later, my mother had been diagnosed with terminal lung cancer. Odd to think now that my formal studies of God were bookended by death and dying. It was Father Griffin, though, who got me thinking about God in a different way, one that gelled with the barren road I was walking on.

The idea of a lonely, forgotten God got me through a lot of dark nights. And it was this God whom I encountered at Eucharist when I heard the priest say what Jesus said at the Last Supper: "Do this in memory of me." My private prayer at Mass most days then was, "Please, God, don't forget me." And I can't tell you how often I heard, in the deepest warren of my heart, God saying to me, "Okay. I won't. But, please, don't forget me either." At Eucharist in those days my sadness found a home in God. It seems to me—a happy melancholic—that Eucharist is always about remembering: remembering what Jesus said and did, of course, but also remembering who we are and *whose* we are. It's about calling to mind the Story, as it is proclaimed at the ambo and the altar. It is a human story that goes to the very heart of a lonely God. Our memory—the repository for all the snippets and chads of our stories—tethers us tightly, gratefully, to this world. Perhaps it also serves as a kind of portal to a deeper truth, a deeper memory: that before we were born, as an old Norwegian myth goes, God took our souls into his hands and kissed them gently. We hold that memory, too, as a gift.

•

One October day in 1980, near sundown, on a deserted stretch of County Road 126 near the California-Oregon border, a gaggle of Canada geese witnessed my father and I commit a misdemeanor. We'd been digging a well at the farmhouse that morning and needed a hundred pounds of gravel. Coming back from the Edwards' farm, where we had returned Mr. Edward's posthole digger, we came upon a big pile of county-owned gravel along the side of the road. My father parked his pickup near the mound and told me to grab the shovel from the back and get shoveling. I don't remember why we hadn't gone to the Fred Meyer in Klamath Falls instead and bought it the way law-abiding citizens did, or why neither of us seemed overly concerned with the wages of sin that day, but there I was—a twenty-year-old aspiring Catholic seminarian (and a future priest) home for a long weekend—shoveling pilfered gravel onto the flatbed of my father's truck as fast as I could while my father—a recently retired lawyer—kept a lookout behind the wheel with the engine on.

A minute into our heist, three or four black-helmeted, tan-feathered, white-chin-strapped geese emerged from the thick tule grass, marched up to the unfenced border of the Tule Lake National Wildlife Refuge across the road, and began barking like junior high hall monitors. *You're not supposed to be doing that*, they seemed to be shouting, loud enough for any soul within a mile radius to hear. Soon three or four mallards appeared and stared at me too; we—my father and I—had apparently become a spectacle. They began yawping as well, their beaks pointed upward as if to help the sound waves along. I stopped shoveling. The waning autumn sun—no longer obscured by a layer of low-hanging clouds—was bathing the mallards' emerald-green necks and their blue-striped silver wings in silky, translucent light. It seemed as if some eternal aperture had been flung wide open and I could see them as God saw them. It seemed I was supposed to remember the curve of their graceful necks, their yellow bills slightly ajar, exposing slivers of pink tongue, and their dark brown eyes that casually took in everything.

"What's going on?" My father said.

"Nothing," I said.

Then I thought twice.

"The ducks, Dad. Look."

"*Jesus Christ.* Jump in back. Someone's coming." My father shoved the truck into gear.

About a half mile ahead, what looked to be a sheriff's cruiser approached, silently. The geese and ducks pecked at tule stalks, dipped their heads in blue water, and murmured like distracted ladies at a church revival. I slammed the tailgate shut, dove onto the bed of gravel, and held on as my father peeled out. As we passed the sedan—its make and model elude me now, but it was decidedly not a sheriff's patrol car—I saw a white-haired man in blue denim overalls gripping his steering wheel. He raised the fingers of one hand—a farmer's salute—as we passed. My father reciprocated with his left hand. He picked at the edges of his right earlobe with the other, a sure sign of a guilty conscience. I'd seen my father picking and rubbing that earlobe before: after being upbraided by my mother for sneaking a snack before supper, for pouring a finger's width more whiskey over his ice than she permitted, and for driving too fast on wet winter roads.

Sailing down the highway now, I looked behind me just in time to see flushed geese lumbering into the air like tiny jumbo jets gaining precious altitude. Cautious and determined, perhaps they were haunted by the memory of the pop and crack, the split-second delay, and the echo of a shotgun's report. They formed jagged, vertiginous arrow tips, honked in chorus—alarm or encouragement, who knew which?—and flapped muscularly. With their flight plan seared into memory, they headed south to rendezvous points thousands of miles away, to lounge and nest. My father and I flew in the opposite direction, I to a quiet evening in front of the television watching football and he to work on a crossword puzzle.

•

The memory of that day spent with my father more than thirty years ago—a pastiche of quacks, honks, feathers, reddened skin, and a dying sun's last blessing—surfaced the other day for no apparent reason. One minute I was gazing out of my third-floor office window onto the academic quad of the University of Portland, and the next minute I was zipping—as through a worm-hole—to the edge of a remote wildlife refuge, where I conjured up, along with the optics of that evening, the distinct musky aroma of a Tulelake autumn twilight, that magical concoction of wheat, clay, volcanic loam, and cool, damp air. I hadn't thought about that day in years. While it might be interesting at some point to figure out why the electric impulses of that memory shot along the tangled circuitry of my cerebral cortex for a midday jamboree in my hippo-campus at that moment, I am content just to have reclaimed again that day: the scent of the sun-cooked gravel, the scraping of the shovel doing its work, the high-pitched honk of saucy geese, the image of my father's reddened earlobe, and the taste of my moth-er's meatloaf (which might not even have been served that night but which nonetheless became part of the memory). It did me good.

I'm betting my blood pressure was a perfect 120/80 and my pulse a tranquil sixty beats a minute that afternoon in my office. At fifty-three and change, I got to sit beside my father when he was the same age. This was a man who didn't make it to fifty-eight, whose name I carry, whose blood flows in my veins, who in life seemed to me unreachable but who in death came to me, kindly, for a few moments. It seemed we were making up for lost time. If I had concentrated, I bet I could have smelled his cheap aftershave. The memory came as a gift: I got to love my father as if he were still alive, still driving his pickup along deserted county roads, still rubbing his earlobe, and still trying to get away with things.

Such memories pop in and out of me a lot these days. A cam-era flash goes off, and for a split second a room lights up and I see a crowd of familiar, distant faces. And then, just as quickly, the room darkens to pitch black, and I am left holding a photograph. If I let it, the photograph will morph into a movie filmed in Technicolor, in which I become, magically, an actor. And then, if I concentrate even more, the movie will become real, as real as the keyboard I am typing on. It's easy for me to see how, as we get older, we can get lost in such memories, these rabbit holes of regret and gratitude. Perhaps we really can travel back in time and have the conversations we always wanted to have, hear again the soothing timbre of a father's laugh, and gaze once more at a sunset that changed our lives. The fact that some memories are at once fleeting and enduring seems to give credence to that old Irish saw about how the past is always present or, as William Faulkner put it once, "The past is never dead. It's not even past."

Even as I relish these vivid memories, I've become a bit uncomfortable these days with what I can only describe as the *flexibility* of my long-term memory. It's become elastic and sticky, I suspect, and thus, I fear, unreliable. I don't wish to get lost in an untrue story. How did my mother's meatloaf, for instance, find its way into that memory of my father and me at the gravel pile thirty years ago? For all I know my mother cooked roast beef. Nonetheless, the memory drips now with tangy catsup on a sizzling, soft brick of ground beef. I suppose I shouldn't be too concerned. Better to add a little spice than to lose the whole meal. It wouldn't be such a big deal except that I want to be able to know when I'm making stuff up. Memory, it seems to me, has a tipping point. Stretch a recollection too far and it will snap. Add one made-up detail too many to a remembrance, and it will, like a house of playing cards, collapse into an indiscriminate heap.

So as my hair thins and grays, my memory has become at times, perhaps, improvisational, and I'm not sure which makes me more anxious. A while back, an eighteen-year-old student of mine (I forget his name) asked how old I was. When I told him, he said to me in a consoling tone—he actually patted me on the back as he said it—"Hey, you're heading into the back nine!" He was referring of course to the point at which a golfer makes the turn after the ninth hole and heads—inexorably, truculently, and with grim resignation (these are my words, not his)—to the eighteenth hole, the clubhouse, a well-earned martini, and a moment to count the new age spots on his hands. I guess I wouldn't mind so much becoming recognizably older as long as my memory maintained a youthful gleam. But it hasn't.

My student's allusion to golf, though, reminded me of those occasional visits home when my father and I would get a round in at the local nine-hole course carved out of a southern parcel of Tulelake farmland. I'm a southpaw, as was my father, so we shared the same clubs. He always made me carry the bag. I never minded. For some reason, lugging those clubs around the course gave me permission to call him "old man," as in, "Hey, old man, your swing is getting rusty!" or "Hey, old man, don't forget to give yourself a triple-bogey!" My dad would smirk and rub his earlobe when I said such things.

After hacking at our golf balls for a few hours (we were terrible golfers), we would sit in plastic chairs on the modest clubhouse patio, watch the surrounding wheat fields turn the color of ripe peaches (in my memory it always seems to be sunset), and drink a few beers. We rarely spoke, and if we did, our conversation turned to safe subjects such as wells and water tables and the weather. I never minded that either. Sitting next to him was sufficient back then. In retrospect I should have used those moments alone with my father to pry stories out of him, pepper him with questions about his youth, and tease out of him details of his life before I knew him. But I didn't know that he would be dead in four or five years. I figured we had time. And I didn't know that his memory was already slipping.

By fifty-three, my father was leaning on my mother's memory more than his own, I suspect. He could never remember where he left his keys, his John Deere cap, the newspaper, or his last will and testament, among other things. Two days before he dropped

dead from a heart attack (my mother told me later), my father went
searching for all of his important papers, including his will. My
mother had to help him dig them out of every closet in the house.
He spent the day putting them all into neatly marked files.

My father in those days couldn't, for the life of him, remember his nine children's birth dates either. Again, he relied on my
mother.

"How old is Pat?" I heard him ask my mother that November
while I waited impatiently on the other end of the phone in my
dorm room.

"I'm twenty-one, Dad," I yelled, but he wasn't listening to me.

"He's twenty-one!" I heard my mother yell from a distance.

"Oh," he said to my mother. "Happy twenty-first birthday,
Pat," my father said to me. Hey, I was grateful he got my name
right.

To be fair, I've never been good with names either. It might be
a congenital condition. When I was a boy I thought my name was
"Brianjackmikegregwhateverthehellyournameis" because that's
how my mother usually referred to me. My father consistently
called me Greg. And I was *named* after my father. Maybe I can be
forgiven then for the faux pas I committed when I was eighteen and
my father was visiting me in my college dorm. We were walking
down the hall on our way to dinner and up ahead a fellow I *knew*
was standing by his door. An accounting major from Hawaii, he
had a degenerative spinal disease I believe, so with his severely
curved backbone he stood maybe four-and-a-half-feet tall.

"Hey, Pat," he said.

"Heyyyyy," I said. I couldn't remember his name if my life
depended on it. I had a recurring nightmare in those days where
I was being tortured. *Just tell us his name* the guy with the brass
knuckles would say. *I don't remember!* I would say. *Just kill me and
get it over with.*

We all stood there awkwardly, as my father waited to be introduced. This is what I said: "Dad, this is . . . is . . . my little buddy."

My little buddy? Jesus Christ. How mortifying still is *that* memory. His name was Don Robinson, by the way. I looked it up in my yearbook a few minutes ago. Now here is an intriguing question: would I be better off forgetting that shameful memory, or do I cling to that memory because it reminds me of some essential truth of my being? I'm not sure. Seeing my father now walking down the hallway with me on our way to picking up my mother at the hotel tells me the memory is worth holding onto. He's chuckling, not in a mean-spirited way, but in a knowing way. The irony humbles me. I am hounded by a memory of forgetfulness.

I sometimes wonder if my short-term memory loss suggests early onset Alzheimer's or dementia, but my doctor insists that it does not. I'm just getting older, she tells me. Memory loss is to be expected, she tells me. She is quick to remind me that dementia doesn't run in my family. But my father and mother—both dead before sixty—died before they had the chance to forget the big things. My doctor is well meaning, and probably right, but her diagnosis is cold comfort. Is this what growing older—growing old—portends? Am I to hear in the fraying of my short-term memory an assuaging lullaby to go gently into that good night? Maybe. But before each forgotten set of car keys, pen, hat, umbrella, book or film or song title, writer, singer, artist, painter, appointment, phone call, or line of verse, I raise a defiant fist that masks a deep fear. I will not go gently into that good night. I will rage—thank you, Dylan Thomas—against the dying of the light. Even as I move steadily toward this dying, this darkness, I will sing by heart all seven hundred words of Don McLean's "American Pie," his elegy to the sudden deaths of Buddy Holly, Richie Valens, and the Big Bopper on that frigid Iowa February night in 1959, almost exactly nine months to the day before I was born, as a way of flexing my memory muscles before some dimming mirror.

It frightens me to think that I might lose my memory some-day. I've seen what happens to those who have. They appear to be almost ghostlike, wrapped in translucent skin. Though contoured clearly by their human physicality, they seem to have lost—along with their memories—themselves. Unanchored, they float in a sea of anonymity. They cry, whimper, and fret. Often they lash out violently. Are they raging against the dying of the light? I'm beginning to think so. I'm also beginning to think that it might be a sin to quiet them with a syringe, a pill, or a Dixie cup of red syrup. Forgotten in a deep fog of unknowing, who wouldn't scream at the top of her lungs in hope of being found? I hope I would.

My father—an inveterate introvert—screamed only once as far as I can remember. I was eighteen. A few days after he turned fifty, my father suffered his first heart attack. When he returned home from the hospital, he wore a zipper of stitches down his chest, a loosely hanging shirt on his skeletal frame, and a raspy voice that sounded almost feminine. He spent those weeks of recuperation mostly in his green easy chair pointed toward the living room television set, too afraid, it seemed to me, to get up and risk exertion, hyperaware of his wobbly heart.

One evening, while I was watching TV, my father sat in his chair working on his crossword puzzle. He tended to talk to himself ("six letters, Hungarian river . . .") while he worked his puzzles, which I found particularly comforting that night. It told me he was still alive and I could concentrate on my show. At one point he stopped murmuring. I looked over. My father was looking at me, or rather through me, to some point far in the distance. He blinked. His reading glasses were perched above his forehead.

"Everything okay, Dad?" I said. He closed his eyes and grimaced.

"Dad—"

My father opened his mouth and bellowed. I'd never heard such a sound, half bark, half wail. His eyes focused and met mine. "I can't. Do this. Anymore," he said between intakes of air, in a frightened boy sort of way. He lifted himself from his chair, threw his pen and the folded newspaper section at me, and went to bed.

"You," he said to me as he reached his bedroom door a few feet away, "go to bed."

Before I did, I looked at the crossword puzzle. In the hour we were together, he had filled in one word.

My father's moaning cry that night still haunts me. It was as if someone had told Picasso he couldn't paint anymore. My father loved words. He relied upon his vocabulary to win over juries and judges. He disdained most adjectives and adverbs; he hunted for meaty nouns and verbs. Now words eluded him, ran from him, and refused to come when he snapped his fingers. Had he, in this mutiny of words, felt his life ebbing, retreating? First you forget a word. And then another, and another, until finally you forget every word. What happens when every word escapes? Had my father admitted to me that night that his life—the collage of words made into stories taped and glued together by memory—was unraveling? I remember now another evening ten years before that haunting night when my father and I sat together at the kitchen table for two hours constructing coherent sentences with my week's list of twenty vocabulary words. In the end, we created one long, elegant sentence using all the disparate words, a feat that later impressed my teacher. At fifty, he seemed to be dangling from the loop of the letter *y* found at the end of some word that was slowly fading.

Without these collected fragments of moments, these pieces of days that we can retrieve and savor and even weep over, if we must, I fear we will no longer know who we are because we will not remember who we were. And if we don't know who we are, what's the point? Memories place us in the middle of a grand story on an impressive stage. My problem is, I'm beginning to forget my lines. And that's no good. I can almost see the long hook inching its way toward me from stage left. So I go deep into a memory, even live in memory for a while, because if I have sprung a leak, if my memories are dripping out of me, then I need to enjoy them while I have them.

Sometimes I forget a person's name or a street name. That's expected, I suppose, but sometimes old acquaintances passes me on the street, and I can't place them at all. In those lonely moments, I recall those Tulelake geese and envy them for their prodigious memory. They had burned into their tiny brains the map pointing out the most direct route from the Arctic Circle to Guadalajara, all the best watering holes along the way, and in the case of those who frequented it, the invisible border of the Tulelake reserve, so they could, with impunity, taunt hunters like my father, who often traveled with a loaded shotgun and a sense of fair play.

And I think of every dog that knows where the bones are buried and of antelope that remember *exactly* the sound a lion makes when it is prowling in the tall Serengeti grass. I know I am not like them. I want to remember what they cannot: what I'm grateful for and what I regret. I know we are hanging on a very thin thread of now, aware that our brief lives are bookended by two silent, daunting eternities. I don't want that thread to snap prematurely, before I have the chance to squeeze every last ounce of life out of every last memory. I don't want to forget anything.

So against the disconsolate drips of leaking memories, I remember the first day of my paper route, a Sunday before dawn with my father driving along my route at a steady three miles an hour, working his crossword puzzle while steering, keeping an eye on me as I run as fast as my nine-year-old legs will let me, back and forth, station wagon to front porches, knowing that the sooner I get done the sooner we get to Winchell's Donut House. I remember later that morning, at dawn, while waiting in line to order our donuts, how my father struck up a conversation with a friend of his. I prayed with my eyes shut that he wouldn't call me Greg when he introduced me. He gripped my shoulder first and then patted my back as he said, "And this is my son, Pat"; I was so relieved that he remembered.

As my short-term memory frays these days, I'm hoping that somewhere deep in my brain—in a terrain one might call the soul—someone installed a memory chip that cannot be removed or erased, one that holds all the ancient stories, an imbedded Ur memory if you like, linking me forever to every human being who's ever lived and who will ever live. But if that wish seems too grandiose, I'll settle for a chip that keeps tidy and easily accessible those memories I have come to cherish, especially those of my father, who looms large these days, as I near the age of his death.

I think there might be such a chip, what Australian Aborigines refer to as "dreamtime," a primordial memory linking us all to the beginning of time itself. I say this because of another memory—for me, *my* most ancient. A few years ago, I was back in my old neighborhood. I parked the car next to my old house. It was autumn because the tree in my old front yard—a tree my father planted before I was even born—was a flourish of red and orange and yellow. The mellow maple leaves blanketing the front yard triggered a memory. I was maybe four years old. In my memory it was a cool, brisk November day at twilight. Sitting on the front porch steps playing with my Slinky, I saw my father's car (a white GTO Pontiac convertible) making its way up the street. He pulled into the driveway, cut the ignition, looked over at me, and smiled. I jumped up from the step as he climbed out of the car. "Daddy!" I said as I ran toward him. As he neared the redbrick walkway, I leaped, and my father swallowed me in his arms. I hugged his neck and detected a residue of aftershave. He held me close as I peered over his shoulder onto a street of yellow-windowed houses. My father kissed me on the cheek, hoisted me onto his shoulders, and took me inside the house. It was the first time I remember my father kissing me.

4. Confirmation

God continued speaking to Abraham, "And Sarai your wife: Don't call her Sarai any longer; call her Sarah. I'll bless her— yes! I'll give you a son by her! Oh, how I'll bless her! Nations will come from her; kings of nations will come from her."

Abraham fell flat on his face. And then he laughed, thinking, "Can a hundred-year-old man father a son? And can Sarah, at ninety years, have a baby?"

Recovering, Abraham said to God, "Oh, keep Ishmael alive and well before you!"

But God said, "That's not what I mean. Your wife, Sarah, will have a baby, a son. Name him Isaac (Laughter). I'll establish my covenant with him and his descendants, a covenant that lasts forever.

God visited Sarah exactly as he said he would; God did to Sarah what he promised: Sarah became pregnant and gave Abraham a son in his old age, and at the very time God had set. Abraham named him Isaac. When his son was eight days old, Abraham circumcised him just as God had commanded.

Abraham was a hundred years old when his son Isaac was born.

Sarah said, "God has blessed me with laughter and all who get the news will laugh with me!"

Genesis 17:15–19; 21:4–6

Holding On

I became a confirmed Catholic when I was thirteen years old, which is to say, I was confirmed at the perfect time. Consider for a moment the gift of the thirteen-year-old boy. (Thirteen-year-old girls, I think, share similar gifts, but I can't speak about them with any real authority.) No longer a child (at least in his own eyes) but not yet a man, he enters the world with newly minted brag-gadocio, tempered by a halting sense of a world that can, if it wants to, crush him. He still cries, mostly in secret, but he laughs, too, and at things he never laughed at before. His humor tilts decidedly toward the silly still, and sometimes the scatological, but he begins to appreciate—because he can—irony, the subtle and not-so-subtle gaffs, pratfalls, embarrassments, and surprises we all must endure in our adult lives. He begins to get it: that life is going to be hard, really hard, and that sometimes the only weapon we have to fend off the creeping darkness is our laugh, our resilient, holy, contagious laugh.

I try to imagine sometimes what that Pentecost day was like, when the Holy Spirit came and lit a fire in the hearts of those disci-ples who were hiding in a dark room behind locked doors. I imag-ine them opening the shades and letting light in. I see them hugging and kissing and dancing. I see them laughing until they're crying. On my Confirmation day, the bishop, adhering to the custom of the day, slapped me (not so) softly on the cheek. *It ain't going to be easy,* he seemed to be telling me. And then he smiled. I stood up and he hugged me. Afterward, when my classmates and I had processed out of the church and to the overflow crowd outside, my sister Sally, hidden from my view by flashing cameras and taller people, shouted out, "Whoo, hoo! Way to go, Pat!" And everyone around me, seeing my reddened face, got a good laugh out of it. And so did I.

•

I enjoy a good laugh. At times, I will snort. It's not that I'm always teetering on laughter's edge; I'm not a comic's easy mark, though sometimes, I'll admit, it feels as if I am. Life, for whatever reason, tickles me. Thankfully though, what makes me laugh has evolved over the years. I like to think that I've become a bit more sophisticated and selective—more Oscar Wilde, less Daniel Tosh—in what I consider funny. So, at best, an ethnic or racial joke, for instance, might elicit a grimace-y upturn on my pursed lips these days.

As a teenager, my asterisk-dotted, dog-eared paperback copy of the *Official Polish Joke Book* (turn it over and it becomes *The Official Italian Joke Book*) often got my buddies and me kicked out of our regular booth at Winchell's Donut House for the cackling racket it always produced. Irish jokes, though, remain in my repertoire for what I think are two justifiable reasons: first, I'm of mostly Irish descent, so I reserve the right to laugh at myself and my tribe; and second, I can produce a passable brogue, a talent not to be wasted. Still, I drag out those jokes only when I am reasonably sure that my audience—intoxicated or otherwise—will not think less of me.

Distracted these days by the thought that the sophomore in me has—far from being tamed—gone rogue, it comes as no small relief that more and more I laugh at uplifting and benign encounters with other human beings. The other day, for instance, I was waiting on my bike at a deserted intersection for the light to turn green when a car sped through the red light. A fellow biker waiting next to me deadpanned, "Wow. That was creative." This made me laugh, which made the droll fellow smile. We pedaled together for a stretch afterward as if we were friends.

I laugh in dreams, which I see as a sign of psychological health. Just the other night, for instance, I had a vivid dream in which I met Queen Elizabeth. (I'm hoping this was because of all the coverage surrounding her recent diamond jubilee.) She had just stepped out of her limousine and was making her way to the rope line where I and everyone else were standing. She came right up to me and (I'm not making this up) asked me to tell her a joke. Here's where it gets weird. I'm now in that transitional state between sleeping and waking. I can actually feel myself being pulled away from the dream. But I tell the joke anyway, even though the queen is slowly retreating to whatever deep warren in my subconscious she inhabits. It begins, "An Irish guy just off the boat in New York walks into a bar . . ." (My favorite jokes, as you know by now, highlight the Irish in their natural habitat.) But that's not the point. The point is, I continued telling the joke. I enjoyed hearing it. It made me chuckle.

I am also happy to report that I still laugh aloud in empty movie theaters. On a free snow day a few years ago while teaching at Notre Dame High School for Boys outside of Chicago, I drove more than a dozen miles in a blizzard to see the musical comedy *South Park: Bigger, Longer and Uncut,* replete with cuss words, fart jokes, and among other eye-popping scenes that only animation can provide, the depiction of Saddam Hussein and Satan as lovers. I, a Catholic priest, obviously didn't want to run into any of my students and thus create unnecessary scandal. Brushing aside the thought that I was probably committing a sin by sitting for two hours in that empty theater along with Kyle, Cartman, Stan, and Kenny, I laughed so rib-achingly hard I am sure I added months to my life.

Outside of my family and a very small circle of friends who love me unconditionally, I admit to very few people my weakness for what I fear are adolescent jokes or movies, because frankly, I care too much about what others might think of me and say about me behind my back. This character flaw drives me a little crazy. I had always hoped that by now I would have been liberated from such nonsense, but to live unshackled is harder than you think. Thus, I can think of few reasons more powerful for dismissing a person like me than the one that haunts me every time I laugh in public, or when it becomes public knowledge that I enjoy what some consider truly tasteless sitcoms such as *The Family Guy*: that he is not a *serious* person, that he lacks gravitas, and that (essentially) he can't be trusted with important matters. This strikes me as unfair and unduly harsh. I think too often we assume the worst about the easily amused. Putting aside for the moment that the object, and not the frequency, of one's laughter might be more telling of one's character, I wonder if we consign the giggler to the gulag of our disdain because in the unconstrained echo of laughter, sometimes we hear the rattling of our own heavy chains.

If the more serious-minded of my religious and academic peers were to somehow discover that I laugh at filthy jokes on occasion; that I can, for lack of a better word, *regress*; and that I never actually grew completely out of the *Mad* magazine stage of psycho-humor development, I would assert—lamely I fear— that Shakespeare was not above diving into the bawdy, too, and that the bard's plays and sonnets are rife with sexual innuendo and double entendre intended to induce titter and cackle, so that even the prudish might finally surrender to that disarming joy that often eludes them. I would remind them that G. K. Chesterton (a serious man) once marveled at Robert Louis Stevenson, who, he said, had found that the secret of life lies in laughter and humility. Stevenson, by Chesterton's reckoning, enjoyed a reprieve from self-importance. He was blessed with that kind of madness that came from the gods, "a divine release of the soul from the yoke of custom and convention" as Socrates put it. Stevenson could look in the mirror, see himself bravely, and laugh. This is what I would tell those whose opinion matters to me and who might wish me to be more subdued. Maybe a little more, and not less, divine madness is called for nowadays.

I say this fully aware that my primary role model in life— Jesus—remained silent on the question of what was worthy of laughter and what was not. None of the gospel writers mentions Jesus laughing at anything or anyone, which strikes me as an odd omission since I have to believe he laughed often. How could he have not? So I say as long as you're laughing *with* someone and not *at* someone—in other words, as long as you're not being cruel— laugh away.

I had always hoped that by now I would have begun to resemble my grandmother, who laughed as I imagined a saint would, that is, with a kind of unselfconscious, childlike delight, one immune to shame or ridicule. She and I listened to Bill Cosby's comedy

albums often when I was a boy, and I was always astonished—
mesmerized, actually—by her percussive whoops, her undulating
belly, her reddening complexion, and the tears that eventually slid
along the deep creases between her eyes and cheeks. Eventually,
she'd simmer down, wipe away her happy tears, and sigh with
the relief we normally associate with those who have survived a
catastrophe. Train your ear to discern the variations of laughter
with the discrimination with which wine connoisseurs train their
tongues and palates, and you can tell when a laugh, such as the
one my grandmother relied upon most, is actually holy. I think that
kind of unfettered laugh is something to strive for, because without
it, I fear we're all doomed.

•

This holy, revealing laughter came into sharp focus for me
the other morning while I was drinking my tea and reading the
paper at Starbucks. A shy, little girl arrived decked out in pink, as
if she had been dunked in a vat of Pepto-Bismol. "It's her princess
outfit," I heard her young father tell someone as he held her hand
in line. The little girl seemed to capture the tension I suspect we all
feel from time to time. Although she wanted to be clearly noticed
for the princess she thought she was, she hid behind her father, a
bit embarrassed by all the attention. Later, while her father sipped
his caffè latte and she nibbled on a slice of cake, the little girl gave
her daddy her rendition of "A Whole New World" from Disney's
Aladdin, as if they were relaxing at home and not in a coffee shop.

I had been reading in the paper about a twenty-year-old boy
who jumped to his death at the University of Washington because
of a lifetime of uncontrolled blushing. So there I was, trying to
wrap my head around what seemed to me to be a totally senseless and preventable death and this little girl who was singing in
a surprisingly well-pitched voice about a magic carpet ride. She
stumbled a few times, conflated sentences, fused words, made
up a few, jumped, skipped, and pirouetted around stanzas, and

in the end slid safely into home. People applauded. The little girl blushed, ran into her father's arms, and tucked her head under his chin. He rubbed her back, whispered something in her ear, and kissed her head.

I turned back toward the window, looked onto the corner of the world that was mine, and thought about that boy who had jumped to his death because of his perennially red cheeks. It struck me as ludicrous, almost laughable, that this world of ours that can accommodate a little girl's dream of royal dignity can also create a person so sensitive to a misdirected or misinterpreted laugh (the article said the boy often blushed when he thought people were laughing at him) that he would rather die than live.

That morning, I think I got the joke the world (the gods, God, the cosmos, etc.) has been telling us ever since the first caveman (or cavewoman) slammed his thumb with what passed as a hammer back then, or outran a saber-toothed tiger, but that most of the time we try to either ignore or deny: we are all tiptoeing on a ridiculously thin tightrope. We are teetering from day to day (sometimes moment to moment) on the razor-sharp edge of calamity and ruin. We laugh, I think, not because we have for a brief moment forgotten how absurd life can be or seem to be but because for one funny, endorphin-producing moment, a gray-suited, banker-type man chasing his hat down the windy street or a little Charlie chomping on his increasingly disconcerted brother's finger reminds us how thin the ice really is. And despite the danger and the seeming futility of it all (and far from deflating us or frightening us), we choose to skate all the faster.

Perhaps this is why Charlie Chaplin movies remain so popular. The Little Tramp mirrors us all. Our grandparents (well, at least my grandmother) howled at Charlie Chaplin's clownish vulnerability, his finely timed pratfalls, and his disarming slapstick and woebegone expressions, because they pointed to a kind of wobbly courage that we all secretly hope we have in the face of seeming futility. Audiences back then weren't laughing *at* him but *with* him. Never was a preposition more crucial to our appreciating the line that separates the cruel laugh from the empathetic. I watched *Modern Times* on YouTube a few months ago and chuckled at the scene in which Chaplin's Little Tramp and Paulette Goddard's character are roller-skating in a department store's fourth-floor toy department. If I had been in a crowded theater, I bet I would have been howling. (We humans, it seems to me, are susceptible to both collective laughter and collective yawning.) At one point (apparently to impress his date), the Tramp blindfolds himself and begins to quite gracefully spin and loop around the department, completely oblivious to the banister-less edge and the four-story drop. I got the joke. I was, I know, laughing at myself.

The Little Tramp's precarious, death-defying roller skating in *Modern Times* reminds me that any day now the existential equivalent of a piano could fall on my unsuspecting head. These pianos are falling from the sky all the time. I'll list a few: being born with pneumonia; finding a dark, oddly shaped freckle on your back that leads to an urgent biopsy; facing a boy with a gun outside a darkened San Francisco movie theater; enduring a head-on crash at the intersection of Nineteenth and Northern Avenue in Phoenix; and hearing that your little brother died the day he was born. And yet, we go on our merry way, dodging all these falling pianos, laughing, and okay, maybe even pretending from time to time that we enjoy a modicum of control over our lives. But then, like one slain by the punch line of a really good joke, we are astonished by one of life's hidden contradictions, which becomes all the more glaring by our missing it in the first place. In tall grass we find a piece of rope we thought was a snake. A friend's tap on the shoulder in the dark nearly dispatches us for good. The more ridiculous or absurd the contradiction, the surprise, or the unexpected encounter, the heartier we laugh, but only if we survive them.

•

Falling pianos make me think of Kafka. Toward the end of his too-short life (he died of tuberculosis at forty-one) and during a particularly rough stretch, Kafka seemed to be equally flum-moxed by both the absurdity of life and our human capacity to, if not transcend it, endure it, and maybe even salvage some scrap of meaning from it. Shortly before he died, Kafka wrote in his diary, "My situation in this world would seem to be a dreadful one, alone here . . . on a forsaken road, moreover, where one keeps slipping in the snow in the dark, a senseless road, moreover, without an earthly goal."[2] By his own reckoning, he was a man incapable of striking up a lasting friendship, incapable even of tolerating a friendship. I would have to read the complete diary to discover why he thought this, but put a little truth serum in most people's coffee and I'd bet most of us would admit to similarly dark nights, when we shud-dered at our capacity for failure, our ineptitude at friendship, or our inability to love or be loved.

And so perhaps we can understand why, as Kafka wrote, he was "full of endless astonishment" when he saw "a group of people cheerfully assembled." It would *seem* (as Kafka would have put it)—given the cold, dark, senseless road that life sometimes appears to be—that laughter is oddly out of place in this world of ours, a madman's giggle, an idiot's titter. And yet, as dire as he thought his life was, Kafka still squirmed uncomfortably at the thought of the darkness, the icy road, and ever having the last word. In the same entry, he wrote, "This brings me to the conflict in my thoughts. If things were only as they seem to be on the road in the snow, it would be dreadful; I should be lost. . . . But I live elsewhere; it is only that the attraction of the human world is so immense, in an instant it can make one forget everything."[3] Forget what exactly? I'm willing to bet Kafka was pointing to the one human situation I've yet to see any comic get an audience to laugh about: human loneliness. It's really hard to dodge that piano.

I wasn't surprised to learn that Kafka laughed a lot, and my sense is that it wasn't a cruel or cynical laughter either. I rather think it was a generous laughter. His friend Max Brod remembered Kafka as a jovial young man, despite his melancholic nature. He apparently reveled in the comic absurdity of life reflected in his characters: the trapeze artist who refused to leave his elevated perch, the hunger artist who starved himself to death, and the young man who awoke one day as a beetle, to name three. Kafka cracked up, Brod said, every time he read the first chapter of his rather disturbing novel *The Trial*. I suspect few readers have found that chapter, let alone the novel, particularly funny. But Kafka apparently did. So did David Foster Wallace, who found Kafka's humor not only *not* neurotic but also *anti*-neurotic. "No wonder," Wallace wrote in his essay "Laughing with Kafka," "[my students] cannot appreciate the really central Kafka joke—that the horrific struggle to establish a human self results in a self whose humanity is inseparable from that horrific struggle."[4] Dire, amused Kafka, Wallace believed, was heroically sane. So when a guy who has lost both his legs to a tractor accident says one day, "You know, I'm half the man I used to be," he isn't making light of his situation or pretending everything is just dandy. Kafka would laugh because the amputee has signaled to him that it is okay to laugh at the darkness. It's the only way we can survive it.

A quick review of some of the subjects Bill Cosby explored in his comedy way back when (which, as I said, often reduced my grandmother to tears) suggests to me at least that Wallace and Kafka, and most comics for that matter, are on to something: brothers being threatened with a severe parental belt-whipping; the biblical flood that wiped out the world (think Japan's recent tsunami writ worldwide); a morbidly obese, speech-impeded boy (Fat Albert); Custer's Last Stand (268 Americans troops dead, 55 injured; anywhere from 36 to 300 Native Americans dead); subway-riding lunatics, winos, and teenage thugs; and spousal abuse (verbal, emotional, and physical). In a crazy world—my grandmother, Cosby,

Chaplin, Kafka, and Wallace would all agree—you can always pick out the crazies. They're the ones not laughing.

Life, though, comes with a laughing rulebook of sorts, doesn't it? One of the rules seems to be you don't laugh about 9/11 (yet), a drunk driver wiping out a family of four, or sudden infant death syndrome. I would include rape on this list, but Louis C. K. and Daniel Tosh have recently broken through that barrier, admittedly with mixed results. Part of me still thinks some comical wells should not be dug. So while the postmodern comic's repertoire has expanded to include the morbidly obese, porn addicts, AIDS, incest, bestiality, and domestic violence, to name just six otherwise sobering subjects broached by one comic I watched with a certain amount of guilty pleasure on YouTube recently (for research), I'll admit that I sometimes pine for those halcyon days of my youth when George Carlin's bit about the seven words you can never say on television created such a scandal.

My dad—who never cussed—didn't care much for George Carlin. "Only weak men swear," he said to me once when he caught me tossing an f-bomb at my brother. I didn't have the heart (or the guts) to tell him then that I had memorized that part of George Carlin's *Class Clown* album and performed it to rave reviews, judging by the guffaws of my male classmates. He wouldn't have found that one bit funny. Nonetheless, I suspect now that my dad probably regaled his lawyer friends with saucy stories and anecdotes over drinks after work. He was raised on a farm after all, sired ten children, drove a muscle car, and drank whiskey. He had plenty of material to work with. It's just that I never saw him in action.

•

I wonder, had he not died of a heart attack at fifty-seven, how my father would have reacted to that day in 1987 when my mother found out she was going to die of cancer. When your mother has just been told the reason she can't breathe is that her lungs are sticky with adenocarcinoma cells, it might not be the best time to try out a particularly dirty limerick to lighten the mood. Thankfully, that's what decorum and the impulse control center of my brain told me as I sat with my brothers and our mother in a hospital room in San Francisco that summer afternoon. And I was the better for my restraint. My mother appeared philosophical upon hearing the news that the cancer was—barring a miracle—terminal. The best she could hope for, if radiation and chemotherapy proved effective, was another year and a half of life. As the doctor droned monotonically, my mother's blue eyes seemed to sharpen, as if the aperture of her lenses were not narrowing in on the white cancerous splotches on the chest X-rays clipped to the fluorescent-lit board a yard away but to a point in the far distance. Her mouth slightly ajar, she had the look of one who was gazing upon a dreamy, gauzy landscape that was, finally, coming into clear focus.

My mother then turned to the open window that looked upon old Kezar Stadium and the northwest tip of Golden Gate Park canopied by a forest of fragrant eucalyptus below and smiled, as if she had just been tickled by a revelation. I knew she was not afraid of dying or of death. But here it seemed that while her inevitable death was no more real to her than it was before the doctor broke the news, her dying was. Perhaps she had nimbly crossed the line we all seem to dread, joined the dying throng marching toward the not-so-distant twilight, and discovered that her hunch about dying—that it's not such a frightening reality, that in fact, dying has a life all its own—had been right all along.

Still, it seemed to me that her diagnosis was no laughing matter. For me, it was as if I had stepped onto a sound stage and was now an actor playing the role of the dutiful youngest son. My brothers and I didn't chuckle, not even once, for the better part of our hour-long tête-à-tête with the doctor as he gave my mother a crash course in radiation and chemotherapy. I took notes on a hospital pad. My mother nodded frequently. We asked lots of questions. At one point my eldest brother asked the doctor if the occasional joint might not be helpful for my mother while she underwent chemotherapy. I looked over at another brother. He raised one eyebrow, but we didn't laugh. My mother did. She chuckled at first. Then, attempting to stifle what clearly was a full-throated guffaw, she simply began to whimper. "Jesus Christ, Brian!" she finally gasped, trying to catch her breath. The doctor smiled cautiously at my mother before turning to my brother. He said that, in fact, when *medicinally applied*, marijuana was known to stimulate the human appetite. My mother let out a shriek. How do you tell this doctor, who knows you only for the diseased lungs laboring in your bony chest, that you caught your son, the future lawyer (and backyard cannabis grower), smoking pot in his bedroom when he was nineteen because your en suite bathroom upstairs shared the same heating duct with his bedroom below, and that when you confronted him, he convinced you to at least try a puff ("How can you knock it if you haven't tried it?"—his exact words) and that you spent the better part of an early summer afternoon in his room toking and laughing and plowing through—as family legend now has it—a case of Hostess cupcakes?

My brothers and I began to laugh heartily. Judging from his raised eyebrows, my hunch is that the doctor was unfamiliar with our tiny acre in the country of laughter. We meant no disrespect, of course. ("Oh, Doctor," my mother pivoted, "I'm so sorry!" She was speaking for her sons who were doubled over in pain.) But then her shoulders began to bob up and down and her torso began to shake. By the time the doctor excused himself, our hands were all over each other as we began to cry in sheer unapologetic joy.

I'm not suggesting that laughter is free to roam where it wills, that it is not subject to the same constraints (maybe a better word is *guidelines*) we impose on tears. There's a time for every affair under the heavens, the wise Hebrew Qoeleth said 2,300 years ago: a time to give birth and a time to die; a time to weep and a time to laugh. Switch those wires and giggle incessantly at a funeral, for instance, and you risk becoming not a clown—who after all, respects the border, however porous, between suffering and joy—but a selfish brute for whom another's suffering becomes his pleasure.

In other words, I don't think I've stepped over the line yet and become one of those people you see careening down sidewalks chortling incoherently to themselves between swigs; but I'm not so quick anymore to write them off as unhinged. I'm reminded of what a doctor told a mostly homeless schizophrenic friend of mine whom I had accompanied to the clinic for a checkup: the fact that he saw angels dangling from trees all the time was because of a chemical imbalance in his brain and not because God was punishing him for all the killing he did in Vietnam. "You might think of it as a gift," the doctor said. "You get to see things—lovely things—the rest of us can't."

Maybe that doctor was on to something. Maybe through the cracks of brittle and generous minds, an illuminating light shines, exposing the comical—if not absurd—state of our existence. If my schizophrenic friend does in fact see angels swinging from trees, I hope—for his sake and mine—those angels are laughing with him, because if they are, maybe, in a sea of gawking pedestrian faces, he won't feel so alone.

5. Matrimony

One day [Naomi] got herself together, she and her two daughters-in-law, to leave the country of Moab and set out for home; she had heard that God had been pleased to visit his people and give them food. And so she started out from the place she had been living, she and her two daughters-in-law with her, on the road back to the land of Judah.

After a short while on the road, Naomi told her two daughters-in-law, "Go back. Go home and live with your mothers. And may God treat you as graciously as you treated your deceased husbands and me. May God give each of you a new home and a new husband!" She kissed them and they cried openly.

They said, "No, we're going on with you to your people."

But Naomi was firm: "Go back, my dear daughters. Why would you come with me? Do you suppose I still have sons in my womb who can become your future husbands? Go back, dear daughters—on your way, please! I'm too old to get a husband. Why, even if I said, 'There's still hope!' and this very night got a man and had sons, can you imagine being satisfied to wait until they were grown? Would you wait that long to get married again? No, dear daughters; this is a bitter pill for me to swallow—more bitter for me than for you. God has dealt me a hard blow."

Again they cried openly. Orpah kissed her mother-in-law good-bye; but Ruth embraced her and held on.

Naomi said, "Look, your sister-in-law is going back home to live with her own people and gods; go with her."

But Ruth said, "Don't force me to leave you; don't make me go home. Where you go, I go; and where you live, I'll live. Your people are my people, your God is my god; where you die, I'll die, and that's where I'll be buried, so help me God—not even death itself is going to come between us!"

When Naomi saw that Ruth had her heart set on going with
her, she gave in. And so the two of them traveled on together to
Bethlehem.

Ruth 1:6–19

Dance Me to the End of Love

A few years ago I witnessed the renewal of marriage vows of a
couple on the occasion of their sixty-fifth wedding anniversary.
Clem wore a grey suit bought off the rack; it hung loosely on
his slightly bent frame, but he still cut a dashing figure. Marjorie smelled of Ivory soap with a hint of lilac, which was how I
remember my grandmother smelling when I was a boy. At one
point in Mass I caught them looking at each other as if they were
teenage lovers. Later, as they stood in front of the altar holding
hands, I told Marjorie that she looked stunning, which she did.
And I told Clem how lucky he must feel to have such a beautiful bride. Clem gripped Marjorie's hand a little tighter. "Father,"
Clem said, in front of God and the whole church that night, "she's
more beautiful to me now than she was the day we were married." I believed him.

Living the sacrament of marriage plays tricks with time and
space. Married love takes two persons and unites them, so that after
a while, you cannot tell where one ends and the other begins. Minutes away from each other sometimes feel like days. Days sometime
flitter away in a heartbeat. Perhaps this is why most of us Christians
are willing to risk everything that matters to us—our own individual compasses; our secrets; our favorite, ratty recliners and stuffed
animals; and our well-oiled daily routines—so we can get hitched.
Every day in a marriage—even the monotonous ones—must be
like jumping out of a plane, a surrendering to a kind of gravity that
draws us back into each other's arms. Unmarried folk, or those like
me—a religious and priest—can only witness such love with awe,
even as we acknowledge that we, too, have our own gifts to offer
the Church and the world.

I recall Clem and Marjorie as I saw them that night and think now of Jesus' farewell discourse in John, and how he hoped that all of us might be swept up by this unifying love—a bond stronger than death. "Father," he prayed aloud for the whole world to hear, "the goal is for all of them to become one heart and mind—just as you, Father, are in me and I in you, so they might be one heart and mind with us. Then the world might believe that you, in fact, sent me. The same glory you gave me, I gave them, so they'll be as unified and together as we are—I in them and you in me. Then they'll be mature in this oneness, and give the godless world evidence that you've sent me and loved them in the same way you've loved me" (Jn 17:20–23). How marvelous it is to be able to say after sixty-five years that your bride is more beautiful now than the day you were married. I want to see the world with those eyes, with that heart.

•

Strictly speaking, I haven't penned a love letter in years. The last love letter I wrote was to my last girlfriend, Maria. Halfway in, I told her I'd finally decided to enter the seminary. I have no idea if she kept that one or any of my other letters, but I've saved all of hers, especially the last one she ever wrote to me, where she closed, kindly, with "I love you, my friend." I took note of that comma. It looked like a long, swinging bridge mercifully connecting two distant, jungled cliffs.

I'm glad that letter in particular made the cut over twenty-five years ago when I, at my mother's urging, sat in the living room by the fireplace and whittled six or seven shoe boxes of old cards and letters down to a manageable three. "Keep only the *important* ones," she told me, an instruction I found a bit unfair. How could I have known at twenty-five years old which letters were worth saving and which were not? Perhaps I was hedging my bets vocationally when I saved Maria's love letters. I don't know. But I'm happy I still have them. They bring into sharp focus a glimpse of my younger self that might have otherwise remained fuzzy and unreliable.

The year before that purging, six or seven months after my father's death and after she had given away my father's clothes, my mother went through her boxes of old letters and tossed those she didn't want into the fire with a detachment that startled me. She seemed to know instinctively which ones were important. But I couldn't help thinking that she intended this divesting of old letters to be a symbolic act of moving on, of letting the dead bury the dead. Every now and then, I grabbed one that missed the fire and inspected its contents to see what was going to be lost forever. I was grateful to discover by the end that she kept my letters, few as they were.

The other day I extracted my boxes of letters from the basement and perused the missives, which number nearly two hundred now. I thought I might get them down to a clean one hundred, but after nearly an hour, I had yet to discard a single one, not even the letter from my college's registrar informing me of my spring semester grades back in 1980. From that letter I mined one particularly enjoyable memory of a teacher I had long forgotten, who, a few short months from retirement, came to class one afternoon sipping beer from a rather large Bavarian stein. At least we all thought it was beer. Every letter seemed to be like that one. They resurrected dead reminiscences, conjured happy ghosts, and plucked distant strings. As I put them in some semblance of order and then back into their boxes, I imagined a grandnephew or grandniece perusing them long after I had died and slowly, over time, re-creating me, at least in his or her mind: a living memory scaffolded by dusty sentences and paragraphs.

I keep my old love letters rubber-banded in one small stack. Sometimes I wonder why. Should I die suddenly and one of my Holy Cross confreres, tasked with going through my possessions, comes upon them, perhaps I want him to know that I intended those letters to be treated reverentially. Or maybe I've tied them together so that at some future date I can quickly destroy them. It's not that they would reveal anything particularly embarrassing, but they do reveal part of me that only a few on the planet are privy to, and maybe I might want to keep it that way.

Before she died, Martha Washington destroyed every letter her husband had ever written to her. Well, almost. Two exist, so far as we know. One, affectionate and brief, has a postcard-having-fun-wish-you-were-here feel to it. The other, written in the summer of 1775, broils with internal conflict, line after line, as Washington struggles to reconcile his duty to the revolution with his duty to his wife and family. One can imagine scores of other letters like it, exposing an inconsistent heart, at once waffling and steadfast. I love the postscript of that surviving letter, in which Washington tells Martha he purchased two suits "of the prettiest muslin." He hopes, he says, that she will be pleased by the fact that he got them at a very good price. In an afterthought tacked to the end of an already personal letter, Washington unwittingly gave the world a glimpse of himself no military dispatch or political speech ever could—of an affectionate, doting, frugal, and perhaps slightly vain husband knowledgeable of fine cotton fabric. No one knows for sure why Martha destroyed all of Washington's letters, but judging from the ones she somehow let slip by, one might be able to guess. Our personal, lovingly penned letters reveal more than we sometimes realize.

Perhaps love letters, then, ought to be kept in a safe deposit box, because they tell the kind of stories never intended for public consumption. I've long forgotten, for instance, what I wrote to Maria when we were dating, but I'm sure my prose was unfettered and, if I can use the word, hemophilic. I suppose if they fell into "the wrong hands"—whose body they might be connected to I haven't the faintest idea—they might prove a little too revealing. But I think I would feel more sad than angry if some stranger were to somehow trip upon them, read them, and laugh out loud. To me, that kind of response would be akin to someone laughing at Rembrandt's *Prodigal Son* or Van Gogh's *Starry Night*. I suppose I see those letters, and the ones I've kept from Maria, as little mas-terpieces intended for an appreciative audience of one.

I'm guessing then that while they might hold onto old love letters, most men my age don't write love letters, unless they're dying, dating, or sneaking around; and if they do scribble a lov-ing sentiment, I'm betting healthy, middle-aged men mostly use the smaller, safer confines of a sentimental greeting card, which is not technically a love letter. Or they text, as many seem to do these days, confident that their electronic, affectionate wisps will evaporate, rightly, into the ether, leaving no trace of authorship. Sitting down with a pen and a sheet of crisp, unlined stationery and actually translating the thumping Morse code of your loving heart into handwritten prose seems to me now not merely quaint (and time-consuming) but also a bit foolish, if not dangerous. Isn't a love letter a bit like open-heart surgery without the scalpel? Isn't that the whole idea of a love letter, to let your beloved see your frantic, pathetic, beating heart? Could this be why Maria's default love letter ink was red? Most of us men who make it to fifty are naturally risk adverse (which helps to explain in part how we make it to fifty in the first place) and so we might be forgiven if we choose to leave love letter writing to those younger men who wouldn't think twice about jumping off a cliff.

Still, at the risk of sounding like my father, I wish to speak on behalf of the personal, handwritten love letter. I hear myself sputtering jeremiads at my younger relations that begin with the lamentable phrase, "In my day . . ." I defend the written love letter aware of the criticism that undoubtedly will be leveled against me—a Catholic priest no less—by my nieces and nephews and all those of the iPhone and droid generation who text with the digital dexterity of chipmunks. I'm willing to wager they haven't put a pen to stationery in years, if ever. When was the last time *you* handwrote a love letter, they might ask. They'll roll their eyes and give me the merest edge of their attention, whereupon I will feel slightly more irrelevant.

Admittedly, I've not yet texted, though my students tell me that texts have overtaken e-mails as the most popular means of communicating for those under twenty-one. Nor have I tweeted or followed anyone's tweets. I understand now my feet are firmly planted in two worlds: the pen and paper world of my parents and the digital world of Generation X, Y, and Z. I am, I know, an immigrant in their native land. It's an uncomfortable straddle at times.

While watching the news a few days after 9/11, I broke down and wept when I heard the recorded voice of a passenger on one of the doomed planes. He told his wife he wanted her to be happy; he wanted her to carry on. And then he said—I'll never forget it—"I'll see you when you get here." I don't think you can find a more beautiful love letter than that or any of those calls made from that plane or the two towers that day. I thank God I live in a world where one last hurried word of love can be shot into space, ricochet off of a satellite, and zing down into your beloved's ear in the time it takes to suck in a breath of air.

Yet, I peruse my old love letters and wonder if, in fact, we've given up too much for the sake of speed. I have letters from my mother when she was younger than I am now; letters from my grandmother written in cursive that tilts decidedly toward the nineteenth century; letters from my brothers and sisters when they were unwrinkled, unstooped, and unstoppable; and letters from old friends, some of whom have died. I read them and get tangled in time and memory. I wonder how anyone can remember anything important about themselves—about who they are and maybe, more importantly, *whose* they are, without boxes of old letters. I don't think I could.

•

I am beginning to understand, though, why the digital natives seem to have turned their backs on the handwritten love letter, relying instead on texts, tweets, and e-mails to share their secrets. Along with Flickr, Blogster, Skype, Facebook, and Google+, these electronic notes promise intimacy without the waiting. It's instant gratification on steroids. Technology has erased (or wants to erase, it seems to me), finally and forever, distance and loneliness. But then I think, why does it seem, at least to me, that despite all these virtual intersections and meeting places, our shrinking, borderless, cyber-connected world has become a lonelier planet? This lonely planet appears to be a wind-whistling landscape of ghost towns with slamming shutters, creaking wood-planked sidewalks, and tumbleweeds.

Nowadays, it doesn't matter if you're minutes or miles apart. We're always together. You can text and tweet and e-mail to your heart's content and never have to make the long trek to the mailbox, never have to wait by the window for the frumpy mail carrier, never have to worry about ink stains and smudges and poor penmanship. I suppose slipshod text abbreviations (LOL, OMG, etc.) emoticons, tweets, and whatever shortcuts will come next, were inevitable. Ever since the creation of the alphabet, ink, and paper, we've been moving inexorably to this moment of instant faux intimacy.

I'm torn. I love the daily stream of photographs and the some-times-truncated conversations going on among my 443 friends on Facebook. The feeling, however thin, that I'm emotionally connected to all of them, is slightly narcotic. I tried to leave Facebook a few months ago; I stayed Facebook-free for a month. Everyone welcomed me back. Still, I can't deny that inner voice (which sounds eerily like my mother's)—sometimes stern but often mournful—that tells me it would be better for my soul if I wrote long letters instead. It doesn't seem so long ago now—though in fact it's been over thirty years—when my mother hastened her retreat from one of my collect phone calls home by saying, "You know, Pat, I would much rather you write me a letter." Her voice reminds me intimacy cannot be had with a few clicks of a mouse.

So the personal handwritten letter has gone the way of the rotary phone, I suspect, just as the rotary phone went the way of the telegraph (which, now that I think about it; was a kind of nine-teenth-century text-messaging machine). In our post-Newtonian world, time and space have collapsed into a virtual here and now. No need for paper or pens. No need for postage stamps. No need to wait. No need to remember. No need to long and pine and fret.

•

I reread one of Maria's first love letters to me the other day. The soft scent of Maria's perfume on the cream-colored stationery sent me back with wormhole efficiency to Mrs. Pecorino's religion class and my pimply, twitchy, and utterly self-conscious seven-teen-year-old self who sat in the third row, oblivious to the lecture, love drunk and nearly passed out from paroxysms of joy, confusion, lust, and pure devotion. God took a backseat that day to straw-berry-flavored lips. Reading that letter, I marveled at the extent to which it played with the space-time continuum. That old love letter didn't so much take me back in time as *erase* time; it brought my past front and center, a feat I suspect no phone text or e-mail could ever accomplish.

Here, of course, I think of that woman who heard her hus-band's message on 9/11 ("I'll see you when you get here"). I sus-pect she has saved that recording and listens to it every now and then for the same reason she has saved all of his letters. She doesn't want to forget the sound of his voice and what that voice revealed.

In stumbling upon Maria's love letter I had long thought destroyed, stuffed haphazardly among scores of old letters, I had stumbled upon a person (me) I thought I had happily left behind. Through her words, a boy, frozen in memory, thawed, sucked in air, and smiled. I could almost feel his hand on my shoulder as he stood behind me, reading over my shoulder. He came to save me. I was not, it turns out, a very shy boy at all at seventeen. Granted, I was no Lothario; Pete Chacon had won that role. But apparently I had—as Napoleon Dynamite would say—skills.

Apparently I was a great kisser in high school. At least Maria thought so. Also, I was apparently really good at giving back rubs and smiling in a way that "brightened" Maria's day. (A smiley face followed.) It was all there in carefully handwritten, red-inked prose. Toward the end she thanked me for my letter from the previous day and begged for another. "I can't tell you how much it meant to me," she said, "that you opened up to me in the way you did." So apparently I told her some of my secrets. Why would I have done such a crazy thing unless someone had written into my genes this propensity for daring that bordered on the dangerous? No other explanation seems remotely plausible.

I put the letter down. My younger self left me to face a hard truth alone: I had gotten it wrong. These many years I had kept out of view this unflattering memory of a self-conscious, dutiful, careful, and insecure boy. But that memory wasn't true, or completely true. Far from being a coward back then, I could be reckless at times, just not fatally so. At seventeen I never did anything outright apeshit crazy. In most areas of my teenage life I went only a few miles over the speed limit—except for one: to the extent that any teenager can, I trusted my heart to someone else. And I put it all on paper. Can any human act be riskier?

She wore my class ring on a chain around her neck that year. We spent hours in her family room listening to her Carol King, James Taylor, and Eagles albums, mostly in the dark. We exchanged hickies, promises, and letters. I remember crying in her arms once. I can't remember what brought it on, but what remains is the image of her cradling my head as I wept on her neck.

Love letters incriminate us in a way that no other letter can. They always seem to expose the wide gap that necessarily separates our younger, foolish, daring selves from our older, more cautious selves. I haven't, strictly speaking, written a love letter in years. I'm a priest after all. But reading Maria's old love letters tells me somewhere that lovesick boy still lives, thank God, the one who gladly slipped love notes into his girlfriend's locker between classes.

•

Mother Teresa, the saint of Calcutta, insisted that, upon her death, her spiritual director destroy the letters she had written to him over decades of correspondence. I can see why. She exposed her deepest secrets in them, and so they count, I think, among the greatest love letters ever written. In one she wrote,

> This sense of loss—this untold darkness—this loneliness—
> this continual longing for God—which gives me that pain
> deep down in my heart.—Darkness is such that I really do
> not see. . . . There is no God in me. . . . He does not want
> me—He is not there.—God does not want me.—Some-
> times—I just hear my own heart cry out—"My God" and
> nothing else comes.—the torture and pain I can't explain.[5]

Years later she wrote in another, "There is so much contradic-tion in my soul.—Such deep longing for God . . . a suffering contin-ual—and yet not wanted by God—repulsed—empty—no faith—no love—no zeal. . . . Heaven means nothing."[6] Mother Teresa went about her day doing good and trying to fend off the darkness. For her it meant preaching hope in dark places. Secretly, she was baring her sallow soul in letters to the one human being she trusted. All those long, damning dashes, denoting doubt and hesitation. They were saved and eventually published. Far from casting her in an unflattering light, those letters—thankfully preserved—introduce us, as if for the first time, to Agnes Bojaxhiu, the woman beneath the blue-striped habit and veil.

Perhaps, as with Mother Theresa, we become accomplices in the demolition of our protected (I want to say "false") selves every time we put pen to stationery and dare to put into writing what we would never utter aloud. Once we mail a love letter, I think it is safe to say, we cede control over our lives, or its cohesive narra-tive, to someone else. The love letter gives the beloved a privileged peek behind the mask. We see the great man in his pajamas, the starlet without makeup. Emerson said such letters were a "kind of picture of a voice"; what a humbling, stripped-down picture it is, and human. At some point, possibly years later, someone—a son or daughter, a grandchild, a distant relative, or the whole world perhaps—could happen upon them and come to know your secret self. I'm beginning to think this wouldn't be such a bad thing.

Maria and I became Facebook friends recently by the way, so I suppose I could go online and ask her if she still has my letters. I suppose I could ask for them back, but that would be rude, akin to taking back a gift. I hope she's saved at least some of them, though, in a shoebox buried in a closet. I think of them now as ancient bones, trace evidence of the boy I used to be. I hope this foolish boy who is willing to jump from high places still lives somewhere inside of me.

●

Someone once said that in most of Winston Churchill's personal correspondence, we never quite know where his id ends and his ego begins. In his letters to his wife though, we get, much to Winston's chagrin, I suspect, his authentic voice: "My darling Clemmie," he wrote in 1935, when he was around my age now,

> In your letter from Madras you wrote some words very
> dear to me, about my having enriched your life. I cannot
> tell you what pleasure this gave me, because I always feel
> so overwhelmingly in your debt, if there can be accounts
> in love. . . . What it has been to me to live all these years
> in your heart and companionship no phrases can convey.
> Time passes swiftly, but is it not joyous to see how great
> and growing is the treasure we have gathered together,
> amid the storms and stresses of so many eventful and to
> millions tragic and terrible years?[7]

No cigar-chomping, irascible, "blood, toil, tears, and sweat" paragon of strength was represented in that letter, that's for sure.

We get "Darling Winston" behind the scowl. But then again, it was a love letter intended for one set of eyes.

Winston and Clemmie saved their letters, but few love letters survive the botched love affair, the fleeting romance, the exhausted marriage. Perhaps the burning or shredding of love letters provides the scorned, the betrayed, the tired with healing catharsis—a wiping out of painful memories—that liberates the wounded, the angry, and the shamed to someday love again. In destroying love letters, though, aren't we, in a sense, wiping out (or trying to, at least) the memory of another whose long shadow leaves us cold, or the memory of one of our (now naive-seeming) selves? I wonder if in the discarding of this inky, tangible evidence of our weak and vulnerable selves we might be sacrificing part of our essential selves too, a self we would sometimes rather forget, given the humiliation that often comes with the memory. I say, save those letters, too. You don't have to read them every day. That would be cruel. But keep them where you know you can find them.

•

My father wrote me one letter his whole life, a few innocuous sentences commenting on a speeding ticket I had gotten when I was twenty. I lost it years ago. Still, I remember how he signed off. "Love, Dad," he wrote. After he died, I searched dozens of closets and basements for that letter before I finally gave up. When I told my mother I had lost it, she hugged me and told me not to worry. She knew my father loved me and told me so. Then, a few days later, she gave me his love letters.

Those letters, written when my father was barely twenty years old, take on Hubble telescope–like significance now, each a tantalizing glimpse of my universe when it was young. My father penned, and sometimes penciled (either way, he wrote in near-illegible, southpaw scrawl), these letters mostly in the middle of the night, before he, a bona fide and dependable summer farmhand, left to cut and stack hay, repair equipment, flood a potato field, or as he wrote one night, dig drainage ditches—a back-breaking job he clearly deplored for the "softness" it seemed to expose, at least to him. "I shoveled ditch yesterday and got 8 blisters on my hands," he wrote (a bit defensively it seems) one night, "and they are so sore that when I write this letter they slowly drip blood." (No evidence of blood can be found on the stationery.) My father apparently was not above a bit of pathos if he thought it would help his cause. To wit, every letter began with a preemptive and sorrowful mea culpa of one sort or another. My favorite was this one:

> Hi, Darling,
> Just finished reading your letter—the one in which you
> bawled me out for not writing—so I'll drop you a line with
> all due apologies for the tardiness and let you know that
> I love you more than ever. I hope that you don't interpret
> these long delays between letters as meaning that I have
> any less love for you. I think of you all the time out in the
> fields, knowing how wonderful it will be when we are
> together all of the time.

Under the thin veneer (thinner than I ever realized) of the lawyer's hide and the thick epidermis of American fatherhood and masculinity beat the nervous heart of young man—a boy barely out of adolescence, really—who couldn't imagine a life without the one woman before whom he never feared exposing his softness. When I first read these letters in 1985 (Robert Bly's *Iron John: A Book About Men*, which got men like my father to go off voluntarily into the woods to drum and share their feelings, wasn't published until 1992), I saw spelled out in black and white on the page my father as he was before he was my father, as he revealed himself to an audience of one, trying on the role of the helpless lover on a new and sometimes daunting stage. In my father's tentative scribble, I saw myself before I was born.

6. Holy Orders

And so this is still a live promise. It wasn't canceled at the time of Joshua; otherwise, God wouldn't keep renewing the appointment for "today." The promise of "arrival" and "rest" is still there for God's people. God himself is at rest. And at the end of the journey we'll surely rest with God. So let's keep at it and eventually arrive at the place of rest, not drop out through some sort of disobedience.

God means what he says. What he says goes. His powerful Word is sharp as a surgeon's scalpel, cutting through everything, whether doubt or defense, laying us open to listen and obey. Nothing and no one is impervious to God's Word. We can't get away from it—no matter what.

Now that we know what we have—Jesus, this great High Priest with ready access to God—let's not let it slip through our fingers. We don't have a priest who is out of touch with our reality. He's been through weakness and testing, experienced it all—all but the sin. So let's walk right up to him and get what he is so ready to give. Take the mercy, accept the help.

Hebrews 4:8–16

Fathers

One of my Holy Cross confreres—a retired priest who is ninety-two and still golfs twice a week—told me a few months ago that he can't believe how fast time is passing. I see him sometimes looking at us younger priests—we who are in our thirties, forties, and fifties—and I think he sees himself as he was only a few years ago. He's winding down, I know. The right side of his face sags, not from a stroke but because some wires have gotten switched somewhere in his brain. So he wears a pirate's patch over his right eye because his drooping eye can't hold in the lubricating tears his eyes naturally produce. Last year they went in and took out a cancerous tumor below his right ear. The chemotherapy wiped out his sense of taste, so he dropped around thirty pounds. He told me once he couldn't figure out why he was still here, and I marveled at that because a couple days before he shot a seventy-eight. I've only shot a seventy-eight in my dreams. So I listen to him any chance I get. I think he's closer to eternity than I am, so I find what he has to say about nearly anything worth listening to. He once told me—because I asked him—that as he nears his own death, things get fuzzier, more mysterious. He said it was as if a hazy veil had come down, obscuring his view of heaven and of God. And then he looked at me with his one blue eye and said, "That's what faith is." I imagined having such conversations with my own father—a decent golfer himself and a man of sturdy faith—but he died when I was twenty-five. Now I'm left to quiz older priests for clues about what awaits me in my autumn and winter years. Hovering nearby—as can only we Irish who see ghosts and fairies in every bank of mist and fog—is always my father, though, teaching me—as an old priest once told me he would, when I was grieving my father's early death—how to love in a deeper, more enduring way.

•

One Saturday night during my senior year in college, I sat across the table from my father in a hotel bar drinking a Long Island iced tea—a witch's concoction of equal parts vodka, gin, tequila, rum, and triple sec with a splash of sour mix and cola—which is devised, I suppose, to get you drunk expeditiously. For me that night I hoped it would give me a little courage. My parents had come up for the weekend, and I had news to tell them, so I needed a little fortification.

"I've made a decision," I said.

"What's that?" my father said. He took a sip from his bourbon and water. I took a long sip from my drink.

"I'm going to apply to the seminary at Notre Dame."

My mother, who was sitting beside me, remained stoic, but I knew she was secretly pleased. Everyone knows that an Irish-Catholic mother prays every night that her son might be a priest. It's their surest way to heaven. No, she didn't betray her feelings one way or the other. She, like me, was waiting for my father's reaction. No one ever told me what Irish-Catholic fathers prayed for every night. If you had asked me back then, I would have said they prayed that their sons would follow in their footsteps. Is it any wonder that three of my four older brothers went to law school, and two of them became lawyers like my father? I thought I was going to be a lawyer, too, until I realized—sometime during my first year in college—I wanted to be a priest.

My father leaned back, as if to take my full measure, folded his arms, and smiled coyly. "Well, you know, there's not a lot of money in that line of work," he said.

"Bill," my mother said, in a tone indicating that now was not the time to kid around. I looked down at my drink and didn't say a word. What my father thought about my decision mattered. I'm not saying I wouldn't have gone to the seminary had my father registered his disapproval. But he was my dad, and I respected his opinion. I wanted him to be happy for me. Perhaps more, I wanted him to be proud of me. I was, after all, named after him.

"Well . . ." my father said. His voice trailed off as if in search of a true word. He patted his belly, filled his lungs with air, and exhaled through his nose. Then he looked at me squarely. He had that soft, almost tender look I imagine he presented to his nervous witnesses on the stand.

"Will you be happy?" he said.

"Yeah, I think so," I said.

"That's all that matters," he said. I smiled. My mother smiled. My father went to the restroom.

I had, up until college, always imagined I would be a father much like my own father. In this, I suppose, I'm no different from most men who as boys glimpse in their fathers their future selves.

We see our fathers as gods when we are very young, demigods until we're around twelve, and if we're lucky, humans when we're thirteen or fourteen. At least that's how it turned out for me. When I was around five I saw my father (a young father of nine) confront a drunken man twice his size at a church picnic. The man—his face the color of a summer tomato—had been berating his wife and his son over something. People at nearby picnic tables were murmuring. My father went and spoke to him softly. From a few yards away I couldn't make out anything my father was saying. His hands remained in his pockets. His head tilted toward the man's ear, as if he were sharing a secret. The man nodded finally and sat down. My father returned, shaking his head, as if he almost felt sorry for the man.

That image—this cosmic force of restrained, masculine strength wedded to simple dignity—stayed with me until I was around ten and saw my own father drunk one night. He got into a fight with his younger brother right on our front lawn and bloodied him pretty good. They sat next to each other on the couch the next morning and watched the Raider game together. Even with a few cuts and bruises, my father retained that morning—in my eyes at least—an elevated stature.

My father became human during my freshman year in high school when my brother and I discovered a couple of *Playboys* in his lower desk drawer one night while cleaning his law office. Up till then, I had viewed skin magazines as the purview of boys who were courageous enough to thumb through them at the local liquor store or crazy enough to steal one by sticking it down his pants when the guy at the counter wasn't looking. Seeing those magazines in my father's desk drawer saddened me. They seemed to suggest that my father might be a secretly lonely man and, in some way, unsatisfied with married life.

Thumbing through the magazines together, my brother and I talked about our father in a whole new way. My brother asked me if I thought Dad had ever cheated on Mom, a blasphemous thought that had never occurred to me. I didn't think he was serious. Absolutely not, I told him, and he agreed. But the fortress had been breached. Before, my father cheating on my mother had been impossible. Now it had simply become highly, highly improbable.

Still, till the day he died, I thought of my father as a good man. He came home every night for dinner, kissed his wife often, and took an interest in his children when it was warranted, typically around the holidays, graduations, weddings, and nights such as the one we shared at that Portland bar. Mostly, though, he kept himself in reserve. Perhaps the thought of doling out steady, if not lavish, attention to his nine children every day exhausted him. It certainly exhausted my mother.

But his quiet nature belied what I have to think was a loud inner life. I say this in part because my father was a Hannon boy, after all, so as with my brothers and me, my father's secret, unruly heart must have, on occasion, kept him up at night. I remember the day when my unmarried teenage sister could no longer keep her pregnancy a secret. She was probably six months pregnant at the time, which might tell you something about our capacity as human beings to deny the truth staring us in the face. My sister told my father she was going to give the baby up for adoption, perhaps as a way to lessen what shame she probably thought she had brought upon his name. She told me later that upon hearing this, my father got up from the end of her bed where he had been sitting and walked out of her room without saying a word. The next morning, my mother told Mary that Dad said that, should she put it up for adoption, he was going to adopt the baby. My hunch is that my father's heart broke that night, not from the weight of shame but from the worry he felt for his little girl.

As a boy I could never mask my shame or worry the way my father could. Neither could I hide my anger or sadness. I cried easily. I never saw my father cry. Only with a great deal of exertion can I mask my tears now. If I find myself sinking into one of my funks, I go off by myself until it subsides, as I imagine my father did. In public, I mask the roiling going on inside me with a straight face. Sometimes, when I feel I'm losing it, I talk to my father, but when I conjure his spirit, he remains mostly silent, which doesn't surprise me.

My father, for the most part, kept his darker emotions in check, and I'm not sure that did him much good. He died from a heart attack at fifty-seven. Aside from a meaty, creamy diet, too many chocolate bars, and his two whiskeys a night, I think he went to his grave early because he kept too much in. He certainly did when I was around. Perhaps he shared his fears, anxieties, and frustrations with my mother. But I'm not so sure. Perhaps this is why, on the day of my father's funeral, my eldest brother gathered us Hannon boys together into a huddle outside the church and told us he loved us—a first for a Hannon male as far as I can remember—and why since then, my brothers and I tell each other before we hang up the phone that we love each other. I think we do this because it's not easy for us to say, and if we can say we love each other, we can say anything. In my father's defense, as my mother told me sometime after his death, he must have figured we knew he loved us because he was in his green chair in the living room every night, ready to give us his kidneys, liver, lungs, or heart if we ever needed them. My hunch is that this was how my father saw his own father.

•

Seven years after that night in that Portland bar, on a February morning, I knelt on the top step of the sanctuary in St. Clement Catholic Church, pressed my hands together as I used to when I was an altar boy, and waited. The pipe organ wheezed. The ceiling fans rotated lazily. Three hundred sets of eyes focused on the back of my head as the bishop came and stood before me. I closed my eyes. He placed his hands on my head and said a silent prayer. Later, I knelt before him again, this time as he sat in his chair. I held my hands, palms up, a few inches above his lap. He dipped his thumb into a small bowl of saffron-colored, aromatic oil; pressed it down into the triangle of flesh between the heart line and the age line of each hand; and made a Sign of the Cross. I watched him as he did this and felt a bit awestruck. Over the years I had used those hands for all sorts of wicked activities: fistfights and bird-flipping and shoplifting to name three. But now they were sacred hands. Holy hands. It began to dawn on me that my life was never going to be the same. My hunch is I felt much like a groom that afternoon, after his bride has slid the gold ring onto his finger. It was sort of terrifying, in a good way. The bishop looked at me and smiled. We stood.

"Peace be with you," he said.

"And also with you," I said. And then he hugged me. In an instant, I became a Catholic priest, a father. The church erupted in applause as I turned and faced them—red-faced, I'm sure. My older brothers stood by their wives and whistled. My mother wept. I imagined my father somewhere between earth and heaven stopping whatever he was doing and looking at me with that coy smile of his, aware—as only one who has completed the long arc of a life can be—that I was in for quite a ride.

Women in hair nets, old men in fedoras, young moms and dads, teenagers, and children learning their letters began to stop me in the supermarket, at the movies, or on the street and say, "Hello, Father Pat." Overnight, I became a father to thousands, millions, billions, actually. Wherever I went, if I wore the Roman collar, perfect strangers would smile and say, "Hello, Father," and I would say hello back, imagining myself saying, "Hello, my daughter" or "Hello, my son," and finding that it sounded too old-fashioned.

•

I have no idea what it means to be a father. To lie awake at night wondering if your baby is breathing. My celibate reality can only imagine this world of fathers. Once early on, after a Mass, a little girl of three or four ran from her father's arms and hugged my legs. She looked up and said, "Father Pat!" and I knelt down and gave her a hug. I had taken dozens of seminary classes in theology and scripture, but nothing prepared me for that encounter. She wasn't my daughter, yet I was her father. I don't recall once as a seminarian a priest taking me aside and saying that I might feel a little cognitive dissonance at being called "Father." How can one be both celibate *and* a father?

Catholics say I am a *spiritual father*, but I have to say, this only makes it more confusing. Does this mean I have *spiritual children*? I suppose they mean that I play a role similar to that of a loving single dad in a household of children. I'm the one you go to when you're in trouble or need advice. I'm the provider, the law, the one who shows up at the big events, the one who sits in the green chair in the living room ready to give you my lung if you need it.

Once, a few years ago, I went to the hospital in the middle of the night to anoint a newborn baby who was not expected to live. I got there within twenty minutes, but it was too late. The baby had died. A nurse directed me to the room where the mother and father—two teenagers, it turned out—were. The mother was holding her stillborn baby, wrapped in a blue blanket, in her arms. The little baby—six months in the womb—looked like a delicate porcelain doll. I stayed with them for maybe fifteen minutes and prayed with them. I offered prayers for the dead baby and left. I didn't cry, though I wanted to. I had no idea what it felt like to lose a baby. I guess part of me felt I had no right to cry.

It seems to me that if I am going to be called a father, spiritual or otherwise, I should have some sense of what it feels like to be a father. But I've never been married and never will be. I've never fathered a child. I've never held a son in my arms the way my father surely held me the day I was born. I've never scaled the side of a brushy hill in a suit and tie on my way to my son's first day of school because my son said it was faster. I've never kissed my teenage son on the cheek at a bus stop as a peace offering after a week of fighting. I've never looked down proudly from an auditorium balcony onto my son who graduated from college. I've never sat with my son across the table in a bar as he told me he was going to be a priest. No, I hadn't a clue what that teenage father felt when he lost his baby boy. I felt helpless as I stood beside him at the hospital bed that morning. My hunch is he felt helpless, too, in his own way, the way a father feels helpless sometimes. I have known loss. But I will never know that kind of loss. And while I am confident I was a good priest to those young parents that early morning, I was nagged then, as I am now, by the thought that I wasn't good enough.

•

My father lost a son once, though we never talked about it. On the Sunday evening of November 10, 1963, I was watching *Bonanza* with my oldest sister in our parent's bedroom. I have no memory of this, but she remembers. She was nine by that time. Apparently we were watching the show on a Magnavox set, which sounds right. Dad was a Magnavox man.

He had a Magnavox console stereo back then that could pan-cake-stack all his vinyl LPs and play them one at a time. He also owned a Magnavox television set in polished dark maple finish that featured prominently in our living room. Coming through the front door every weekday at 5:30 from a long day, Dad would set his briefcase on top of that TV, take off his coat and drop it on the couch, loosen his tie, lower himself into his green leather chair, stretch out, and cross his legs at the ankles on the matching ottoman. He would let out a long sigh, like a Jake-braked diesel releasing pent-up compressed air, and then a few minutes later belch predictably. That belch seems now to carry with it alpha-male significance. He would tell whoever happened to be watching the television to switch to Cronkite. He would snap open the evening paper and read. Sensing one of his older boys slipping past him, he'd say in a tone not unpleasant or unkind, "Go make me a drink," and the boy would deftly diagnose his father's mood and measure out the bourbon with an eye toward either lifting his spirits or maintaining them right where they were. Three fingers of bourbon was always a safe bet.

So, while I was splayed on my parents' bed upstairs watching *Bonanza*, Dad was probably downstairs watching his Magnavox and sipping on his second bourbon. It's hard to say what he was watching because on weekends we rarely saw each other anyway, except for the Sunday-morning paper routes, which he drove me and my brothers on; morning Mass, which I slept through anyway; and the dinner table, at which my father occasionally sat, wide-eyed, as his children descended like hyenas upon Mom's meatloaf.

But that Sunday evening and early Monday morning in November—the day before and of my fourth birthday—were different. At some point during that nine o'clock evening hour, Dad told my sister and me he was taking our mother to Eden Hospital. Mom was going to have the baby. Sometime that night or in the early morning of the next day, the baby, James Joseph, died: umbilical cord around the neck; asphyxiation in the womb; stillborn (what an odd euphemism). And while it would be years before my mother could bring herself to talk about it—and when she did once, her lower lip quivered—the only thing my father ever said about the ordeal is what he told us that morning as he woke up the five older ones for school and we three younger ones for breakfast. "The baby died," he said. By my recollection he never spoke of James Joseph again. Every tiny detail of that night seems burdened now with meaning.

Looking back, it had to have been the most painful day of my father's life. Admittedly, he was only twenty-five when his father died in a farmhouse bed. (Only now do I realize that this, too—our age on the occasion of our respective fathers' deaths—we share.) But he had a wife and a child and one on the way back then, and his father had been sick for a long time. Losing a parent can be hard, but how does a father or a mother lose a child and go on living? Pain that cannot forget, Aeschylus called such moments of

grief. Pain that falls drop by drop upon the heart. I never asked my
father about the unbearable loss he must have felt that day. By the
time I had worked up the gumption to ask, when I was twenty-five,
Dad had had his second heart attack and died. I think now that if
I could go back and ask him—or better yet, watch him—he would
tell me something important about who I am now, a lawyer's son,
a Catholic priest who answers to *Father*. But I can't.

A worn Kodak snapshot taken around that time offers a clue.
It shows my father standing iron-rod straight in a dark blue suit,
shoulders square, and his left hand cupped smartly at his side.
His right hand rests on my tiny right shoulder; his fingers seem
to be pressing into my shoulder blade, as if he's holding on. I am
standing below him, tucked against his long legs, in my dark blue
suit, white button-down shirt, and clip-on tie. I am smiling for the
camera, my eyes squinting into the sun. The palms of my hands,
rosary-draped, are pressed together at my chest as if in prayer. It
is the morning of my First Holy Communion. Dad is smiling but
only barely. Tightlipped, his smile curves slightly upward on the
right side, a tiny comma. Maybe I'm just reading this into his smile,
but it looks as if he's just going through the motions, as if his life
among nine children was nothing more than one continual photo
shoot. *Come on, Dad. Smile!* What if—as I suspect now—it was more
than that? What if two and a half years after James's death, he was
still grieving and was only forcing a smile? What if smiling was
the last thing he wanted to do?

I think if you look at my First Holy Communion photograph
closely, you will see what I see. Two years after the death of his
baby son, he's standing on the front lawn with his youngest *living*
son and he is smiling. But look closer. His eyes betray him. They
seem to be the eyes of a grieving man. He's still hurting. He must
be. I know he wants to be happy for me. I know that if I were ever
caught in a burning building he would rush through the fire and
save me. I know he loves me. I'm sure of that. But I'm pretty sure

now he didn't feel like smiling then. I think he wanted to cry for the boy he lost. But I don't think he knew how.

An early, gauzy memory: Sometime that November morning in 1963—the day my little brother died—I walked up steep, almost perpendicular Arcadian Drive by myself. Four-year-olds in my town enjoyed a less tethered existence in those days, I suppose. At the top of the hill, our street abutted a large hilly field. Thirty or forty feet beyond the last house, tucked away in tall weeds and tree groves, was an enormous boulder, a rock sufficient to hold four or five kids. I scampered to the top of it and sat. I was a tiny, enfogged Thinker. A chilly mist. A darting mud swallow. Silence. A field thick with phantoms, most of them Japanese kamikazes, as I used to think back then. I must have contemplated all sorts of things as I sat there. At one point I said out loud, "The baby died." To this day, I don't know why I said it. Was it because my father had, and I was already, at four, beginning to mimic him?

That morning, after he had secured a babysitter for my younger sister and me and dropped the older kids off at school, my father visited my mother in the hospital. He sat with her for half an hour and then put in a full day at his law office. I know this because I have his appointment book for 1963. He wrote it all down.

•

On my ordination day, before the bishop laid his hands on my head, anointed my hands with sacred oil, and made me a father, he asked me to lie prostrate in the main aisle of the church. Try it sometime. You'll feel a little naked, exposed. I rested my head on my hands in front of me; my nose touched the carpet. The choir led the congregation in the chanted Litany of Saints. It began first with everyone asking God—Father, Son, and Spirit—to have mercy on us. Then, starting with Mary, and proceeding to the archangels and apostles, they asked, one after another, all the saints to pray for us. I know, though, that the congregation was calling upon those dozens and dozens of saints, some of whom I'd barely heard of (who *are* Saints Gervase and Protase?) to pray for *me*. God knows I was too.

While the church was chanting, I listened with my eyes closed. I was thinking of my father. I was wondering where he was, *if* he still was. My heart pounded, a drumbeat of joy and sadness. I wanted my father to be there. I had always imagined that we would grow old together. I had always imagined my father showing me how to be a father as he had shown my brothers in their early years of fatherhood. But he was nowhere to be found.

Old priests that I admire say celibacy is a gift, and I believe them. Perfect strangers, parishioners, and students of mine tell me things they would never tell their closest friends, their spouses, or their children. In my untethered, unmarried life they see, apparently, an opening wide enough to carry their secret burdens. I greet them when they are born, watch them grow, absolve them, and feed them. I'm there when they are sick and when they die. Mine is a privileged life, and I am grateful for it. But the babies I baptize, the students I counsel, the couples I marry, and the men and women I feed at Eucharist, absolve in the confessional, anoint when they are sick, and bury when they're dead are not, really, my children. I am their priest, and they call me father. But the title is, I know, a sign of affection and respect, and nothing more.

Still, I want to know what it feels like to be a father without having to go out, get married, and father a child. I'm not crying out in loneliness, but for some strange reason, I have this thought that if I can feel in my bones what good fathers feel, I will be a better priest. And since most men learn the lessons of fatherhood from their own fathers, I will catch my father now in an unguarded moment back then, when on arguably the most painful day of his life, he lost his baby boy, and listen to what he has to tell me. I will not in my imagination have him do what he would not do in real life. I will not have him cry if he cannot or does not wish to.

•

As my father drives down the steep slope of Arcadian Drive on his way to Lake Chabot Road and the hospital a couple of miles away where he will walk my mother to the emergency room, wisps of coastal evening fog cling to autumn birches and maples and redbuds. My father's left hand grips the steering wheel, and his right hand massages my mother's neck. In my imagination, Ray Orbison's "Only the Lonely" is playing on the radio.

At one point Mom senses that something is wrong. ("I told the doctor 'The baby needs to come out,'" my mother will tell me years later, "but he said no. He said we had plenty of time.") As they pass Romley's Market and Carl's Drugs halfway to the hospital, Mom looks at Dad and tells him he better hurry. He steps on the accelerator gently. I watch Dad driving down Lake Chabot Road in the red Ford Falcon station wagon (nicknamed "Lightning" by us kids) on the way to the hospital that November night. I observe the faintest hint of panic in his eyes, and this surprises me. I have never seen my father's brow furrow like that. He steps on the gas more. He knows my mother and the clipped tone she employs when she is serious, the one that brooks no discussion, not even from him.

As he sits in the maternity waiting room that November evening, Dad is reading the newspaper for the distraction it provides. I see my father sitting straight up in the lounge chair, alone in the room. He folds the newspaper into a roll and begins tapping his knee with it. He stands up and begins to pace. I can hear his heart beat faster in his chest. He sits down again and puts his head between his legs. The long fingers of his tanned hands massage the back of his knotted neck.

It is two, maybe three, in the morning of November 11, my birthday. My father jolts to attention when the door that leads to the long corridor that leads to the operating room opens. The surgeon in green scrubs approaches him. He speaks in medical jargon. The baby had a nuchal cord, that is, the umbilical cord was wrapped around his neck, which is not uncommon. Sometimes the cord can compress and the oxygen delivery to the baby is compromised. Compromised. It sounds eerily like military speak. The baby was stillborn, the doctor says, and then he gently touches my father's shoulder. For a moment, my father cannot breathe. He asks if he can see his wife. The doctor says of course, a nurse will be by to take him to her room, once she is settled in. My father stands in the middle of the room, his hands dug deep into his front pockets. He stares at a point far away. He is alone. He is not crying. His eyes dart left and right as if he's looking for something to hold onto. For a brief flash I see my father stripped to the bone. His heart dips, ebbs, pulses, lurches, and swings within its osseous cage. And I think to myself, he is crying after all. You just can't see it.

That evening, my father sits in his green chair. I am sitting with him, a man of fifty-four, but he sees only the boy I was then. I ask him if I can make him a drink. He says sure, and I get up and make my way to the kitchen. I look back. My father is watching the news. He's absorbing the world in all its absurdity and wonder, with a huge hole in his heart none of his children will ever see. Tomorrow, I know already, he will get up; shower, shave, and dress himself; make breakfast for his brood (which we all hope will be hot chocolate and toast coated thickly with butter); and drive the older kids to school while leaving the youngest of us in the capable hands of our babysitter. He will visit my mother in the hospital and go to the office, where he has scheduled four morning appointments and five afternoon appointments. It will be a full day, so I decide to be generous as I drop three ice cubes into a short glass and reach for the bottle of bourbon.

7. Anointing of the Sick

Are you hurting? Pray. Do you feel great? Sing. Are you sick? Call the church leaders together to pray and anoint you with oil in the name of the Master. Believing-prayer will heal you, and Jesus will put you on your feet. And if you've sinned, you'll be forgiven—healed inside and out.

Make this your common practice: Confess your sins to each other and pray for each other so that you can live together whole and healed. The prayer of a person living right with God is something powerful to be reckoned with. Elijah, for instance, human just like us, prayed hard that it wouldn't rain, and it didn't—not a drop for three and a half years. Then he prayed that it would rain, and it did. The showers came and everything started growing again.

My dear friends, if you know people who have wandered off from God's truth, don't write them off. Go after them. Get them back and you will have rescued precious lives from destruction and prevented an epidemic of wandering away from God.

James 5:13–20

Superman

We end our days on the planet—if we're lucky—as we began: "Sans teeth, sans eyes, sans taste, sans everything" as Jacques puts it in his famous "All the world's a stage" speech in Shakespeare's *As You Like It*. He called those last days a "second childishness" and mere oblivion. The sacrament of Anointing of the Sick celebrates this often uncomfortable truth about our mortality. Death awaits us all. I've anointed babies in intensive-care units as their mothers and fathers looked on in horror and hope. I've anointed toddlers and teenagers fighting leukemia. I anointed my mother several times in the last months of her life and once on her last day. And last spring I anointed a ninety-eight-year-old nun dying in her convent bed. (Her confession a few minutes before began with, "Bless me, Father, for I have sinned; this is my last confession.") As I marked her forehead and then the palms of her hands with an oily cross, she appeared to me translucent, a feather ready to float.

In the old days we called it Extreme Unction or Last Rites, because back then, you waited until all hope was lost before you called the priest. You expected to die before the oil on your forehead and on the palms of your hands had a chance to dry. Now, priests anoint anyone who asks for the healing oil, which suggests, it seems to me, a move in the right direction. The oil of the sick is, after all—like sacred chrism and the oil of the catechumen—an oil of gladness, in its own way, that marks us with hope as we begin our march through whatever dark valley awaits us. It steels our spines, strengthens our shaky knees, and reminds us that we do not walk alone. Most of us—if we are lucky—grow up believing that we are invincible, that with sweat and moxie and imagination, we can achieve immortality of one sort or another. And then, at some point we become acquainted with a sobering truth, that, as Hemingway put it, "the world breaks everyone and afterward many are strong in the broken places." What a lovely gift, this healing oil that is offered to us when we have, at last, been brought to our knees in defeat. This glad oil mixes graciously with our tears, our wounds, our fears, and our brokenness.

•

I watch television more than I probably should. I find that I watch it most when I don't want to be around people. I'm reminded of the beginning of *Moby-Dick* where Ishmael says that when he's in a real funk ("whenever it is a damp, drizzly November in my soul; whenever I find myself involuntarily pausing before coffin warehouses, and bringing up the rear of every funeral I meet"), he figures it's time to get back to the sea. Maybe that's what television is for me: a faraway yet familiar place to go to when I am beginning to despise myself and figure there's no reason for anyone else to like me either. Instead of boarding a ship, I lie on the couch, grab the remote, cover myself with a blanket, and begin flipping through the channels.

I remember one particular Saturday a while back. I can't recall exactly now what dark thoughts had pinned me, but I watched television the whole day. I got lost in one show after another. I had lunch, I think, and stayed hydrated, but from eight in the morning until well after midnight, I remained curled up on the couch and switched from one channel to another, avoiding every commercial. Once, on a particularly bad day, I sat and watched the entire *Lord of the Rings* trilogy. I must have been in a serious funk then, but then again, I'm sure watching Frodo save Middle Earth probably did me some good that day.

Why is watching television my default activity when my soul turns decidedly chilly and autumnal? This goes against everything I've ever read about what to do when you feel depressed (or melancholic, as I prefer to describe my condition). Dr. Phil, WebMD, my spiritual director, and my mother when she was alive all say (or said) that when you're feeling down, you should go out and do something, anything: take a walk, go to the gym, call up a friend, or go to a movie. Bake cookies. Change the oil in your car. Do something constructive. Sweat. Sing. Read a book. Don't isolate yourself, they say. Closed drapes and television only deepen the darkness.

Or, if the sadness becomes overly oppressive, they say, go to the doctor. Get some medication. Unfortunately, I've closed off this avenue to better health. I try to stay away from doctors, except for my yearly checkup, which, if I'm truthful, happens every two years. And I don't like taking any medication if I can help it. I'm particularly skeptical of painkillers of any sort, especially psychotropic drugs such as Prozac. I'm sure they can be helpful, even lifesaving sometimes, to the severely depressed, but for occasional melancholics such as me, a few hours of alone time before the television often do the trick. No, I prefer to tough it out when I'm in one of my dark moods, which means staying away (if I can) from others until the fog lifts. So, in the end, I've got my television, a reasonably decent-sized, flat-screen number that takes up a dominant spot in my tiny living room.

As a college professor and Catholic priest, it's convenient, I suppose, that I usually get my deepest funks on Friday afternoons. By Sunday morning, I'm usually my old self again (or pretty close to it), sufficiently energized for saying Mass and preaching, and for teaching my students writing on Monday. It's as if I've trained myself to wait until Friday night to become disgusted with myself, so that I can spend a good part of Saturday being alone, trying to figure out why I so dislike myself at times, while watching *Leave It to Beaver* or *Petticoat Junction* reruns. Or I'll watch the Game Show Network for a few hours, get tired of *Family Feud* at last, and switch to MSNBC and watch a few hours of *Lockup*, the prison documentary series.

When I'm in a deep, deep funk, I'll watch *Cops* on Fox or *Police Women of Broward County* on TLC for a few hours, but even *I* realize that watching those depressing reality shows will leave me feeling worse. Still, sometimes I can't help tagging along with police officers to the most dangerous neighborhoods in Detroit or Miami at midnight and become a voyeur to the heartbreaking lives of the working poor, drug addicts, and prostitutes. I see them looking at me through the camera lens; you see that they are mostly humiliated, exposed to the world for the caught, broken creatures they are. But even then, you see a suspect shielding his face from the klieg lights and cameras or gathering his pants up; you see her pushing her much-too-short skirt down to cover more of her legs or fixing her hair so she will appear more dignified, and that makes you feel a little better for having spent an hour watching sadness take on human flesh.

Mostly, though, I gravitate toward the MeTV network these days (the "Me" stands for "Memorable Entertainment"), where I watch all the shows I grew up on. My favorites are *My Three Sons*,

Leave It to Beaver, Father Knows Best, The Rifleman, and *Dennis the Menace.* Honest to God, sometimes I think I could watch those shows all day long. They are, for me, the mac and cheese of my television diet.

As a priest, when the darkness comes on the weekends, I feel doubly disadvantaged. While it's true that for a priest there's no such thing as a day off, Saturday comes closest to it. On Saturdays, I can often sleep in, piddle around my apartment, not get dressed until noon, and be the person no one gets, or has, to see. I love Saturdays for the wide range of options they usually provide, so when I spend nearly the whole day watching television because I can't imagine stepping into the real world, I end up feeling like a pretty lazy lout, which is not exactly how I want to feel the day before Sunday. I will get up on Sunday, though, and usually feel better, good enough to say Mass and preach. This always amazes me. No matter how dark Saturday was, no matter how much television I watched or how much time I spent holed up by myself—feeling so unlovable that being alone made complete sense—by Sunday, I usually feel better. Maybe I've trained myself to feel better by Sunday.

What role does watching television play in this tragic-comedic drama I call my life? Is it possible that television provides a kind of therapeutic balm to my tired brain? I'm suspicious of this possibility, because it seems to me that of all the activities I consider healthy (exercising, eating well, getting sufficient sleep, spending time with friends and family, reading, etc.), watching television by myself for hours on end doesn't come close to making the list. I'm sure this is the reason many psychologists these days note with alarm the unhealthy amount of time young people seem to spend playing video games. On a video-gamer bulletin board, "Husvarneque" said,

> Hmmm . . . let's see, been playing games since I was . . .
> six, I'm sixteen now . . . ten years, average eight hours a
> day . . . 3650 days . . . multiply. . . . So about a total average

of 29200 hours (1216.6666666667 days) in total across my
entire lifetime. As for each console specifically, couldn't do
it . . . but I've played the super Nintendo, N64, Gameboy,
Gameboy advanced, PSone, PS2, Xbox, Xbox 360, and PC
games . . . soooo . . . yah.

I think this kid is speaking for his generation, or at the very least,
wants to.

Psychologists said the same thing about television for those
of us who grew up before Pong and Asteroids, when they noted
the ungodly number of hours we spent watching television every
week. Perhaps they're right. Perhaps staring at any screen for hours
at a time (computer, Smartphone, laptop, tablet, television, and
movie) is ruining us. Perhaps our singular devotion to these screens
has become more palliative than life-giving. At the very least, they
say, we ought to be interacting more with those of our own species
than with fictional characters, virtual beings, or computer-gener-
ated avatars, however enticing they may be.

Perhaps this is why my mother often had to push me outside
with a broom on summer days when I was a boy. "Go outside and
play," she would say with more than a hint of exasperation in her
voice, "and don't come home until it's dark." So I would trudge
outside and catch up with my friends Boober, J.P., and Babe Willis
at the baseball diamond the older boys had carved from a field of
knee-high weeds at the edge of our neighborhood. They would be
sitting on Caviglia's backyard fence watching the older boys play,
and I would join them there. Every so often one of us would yell,
"Hey, guys, let us play for a change," and the older boys, including
my older brothers, would laugh, shake their heads, punch their
mitts, and continue playing. Once, I got so mad at their dismissive
shoos (I had imagined myself to be a great baseball player back
then) that I took a bat and flung it at them. It hit one of the boys
square in the head and knocked him out. I ran away as fast as I
could and hid for the rest of the afternoon in the crawl space under

our stairs, convinced that I had killed him. My mother eventually found me and made me go back and apologize.

My mother kept pushing me out into the world, but mostly I was content to sit in front of the television on summer afternoons and watch my favorite shows. I know I often like to think that I spent most of my childhood riding my bike, playing at the park, or hanging out with my friends in one of the tree forts we had built and abandoned over the course of many summers, but truthfully, I clocked impressive hours of television time back then. If I wasn't eating, sleeping, working my paper route, or bowling, I was probably splayed on the living room carpet three feet from the television watching *Superman*, *Dragnet*, *Lost in Space*, *Dark Shadows* (four favorites), or whatever happened to strike my fancy. My brother convinced my parents one year to let us buy a small, used, black-and-white television with our paper route money. I gladly became the channel changer for my brother that year just to experience the unmitigated joy of watching television from my bed. At the time, I didn't think life would get any better.

I have to believe that I was not unique in my devotion to television back then. Coming home in the early evening from delivering the afternoon paper, I often passed the houses in my suburban neighborhood, nearly salivating at the flashing blue lights emanating from their living room windows—the telltale sign of hot cathode ray tubes translating electronic beams into pulse-quickening dramas—and pedaled home all the faster. I didn't want to miss out on what everyone else was watching. Back then, I thought the whole world was watching television during prime time.

Sometimes these days, after having stayed up too late watching a *Columbo* or *Love, American Style* rerun, I console myself with the thought that, had Lincoln been alive during the television age, he, too, would have vegged out in front of his television, though it's hard for me to imagine Lincoln in a Snuggie noshing on Pringles while watching Honey Boo Boo, the Kardashians, or the Real Housewives of New Jersey (which, for the record, I don't). He would have camped out at PBS, I suspect, or the Military Channel. I didn't ask to be born into a television-saturated culture, but I was. Every age has managed to fashion for itself diversions of one sort or another, haven't they? Late afternoon strolls, front-porch storytelling, parlor games, public readings and debates, dances, musical recitals, books, sporting events, carnivals, tent revivals, radio shows, movies, television, computer games, video games, Smartphone apps. Who's to say that one is necessarily better than another if each, in its own way, satisfies someone's need to take a short break from reality?

The truth is, when I'm feeling fine, I don't actually watch a whole lot of television. In fact, on my good days (which outnumber my bad days probably six or seven to one), I hardly ever turn on the television. I do have my daily routine, though, which has me watching *The $25,000 Pyramid* (the old one hosted by Dick Clark and not the newfangled, boring one on now) while having breakfast; watching a half hour of Judge Judy when I get home from work; and falling asleep to Conan O'Brian. And I do have my couple of shows I can't miss: *Modern Family* on Wednesdays, *Boardwalk Empire* on Sundays, and English Premier Soccer on Saturday mornings. That's about it. On my good days, I take my morning walks, go to the gym, have a beer with my friends at one of fifty microbreweries in the greater Portland metropolis, and pray.

So, since I grew up watching television, perhaps I should not be surprised that when I am uprooted, disjointed, tangled, lost, or completely exhausted by my life and me in it, I run to the television. For a while I don't have to think about anything or anyone. I don't have to think about myself. I can get lost in someone else's story, even if it's fictional. For a blessed few hours I can imagine growing up in the late 1800s with a single dad in North Fork, New Mexico Territory, with my own horse and gun; on bucolic tree-lined Mapleton Drive circa 1960, dotted with picket-fenced ranch houses and populated by thoughtful neighbors and dependable cars; or in Bryant Park, a town over, that looks like what I imagine

Los Angeles looked like when I was a child growing up outside of Oakland, before LA got too crowded, smoggy, and smug. I can go to these places that feel familiar to me and rest. Thirty minutes later, I sigh with satisfaction. Once again a serious obstacle has been overcome, a conflict has been resolved, and all is well with the world. Sometimes I can't get enough of those stories.

•

As a boy, my favorite show was *Superman*. I was so enamored by Superman then that I had my mother sew a red cape (a large beach towel) onto a blue shirt of mine on which I had painted a white S. We had so much in common back then, Clark Kent and me. We both wore glasses. No one took us very seriously. We both knew we had secret powers, and both of us bore the weight of great responsibility to use those powers unselfishly. We both knew that we were sent to Earth to save it. So you might imagine how amazingly fantastic I looked when I put on my homemade Superman outfit: the towel-festooned tee shirt emblazoned with that huge white S, a pair of red shorts, white socks, and my PF Flyers. I would leave my glasses on the kitchen counter and run outside into the street convinced that, like Clark Kent, no one would recognize me without my glasses on. I lived for those moments of hidden greatness, those times when I began to appreciate the power and the burden of irony. But I slept better at night knowing my neighborhood felt safer for my having patrolled it on those Saturday afternoons as its one and only man of steel.

I don't know. It seems a bit silly now to suggest that television played such an important role in my life back then, but it did. There's no way I would have run outside, even at five years old, dressed as Superman, if I hadn't actually believed that no one would recognize me without my glasses. Watching *Superman* every day got me so enmeshed in Clark Kent's story that, for whatever reason, his story became mine. I could relate to Clark Kent's daily predicament, his burden of being secretly someone very important

and powerful, and how he had to hide his true self (and one particular weakness) for the sake of others. I think Clark Kent gave me
permission to be lonely in my dreaming sometimes without being
overwhelmed by the loneliness. I think I began to understand why
no one, including those who thought they knew him best (here
I'm thinking of Lois Lane and Perry White and *not* Jimmy Olson)
appreciated him for who he was. The world is generally unkind to
small boys who wear glasses; it tends to laugh rather dismissively
at those who imagine themselves to be greater than they appear
to be.

It's interesting to consider which came first: my sense of
myself as someone vitally important or *Superman*. But clearly by the
time I went to school I had the sense that I could do anything if I put
my mind and heart to it, that I had a deep reservoir of power within
me that I could tap. Superman could fly, see through walls, bend
steel with his bare hands, and so forth. My power, it seems to me,
was my imagination. I could imagine myself doing great things,
though (or because) I was a small, thin boy with thick glasses.

In the fourth grade I imagined myself as an architect. I would
be not just any architect but a great architect. While my brothers
fought over the sports page on Sundays, I explored the perennially ignored real estate section that had simple, architectural floor
plans of new houses that were presently on the market. I studied
them, unlocked the code of their architectural design, and then, on
Sunday afternoons, spent hours at the kitchen table designing, on
sheets of white paper, million-dollar houses of my own. I was going
to be a brilliant architect. Then one day, Tim Quinn (who sat across
from me in school) announced that he was going to be an architect
and showed me the architectural tools his parents had bought him:
pencils of various thicknesses, special rulers and paper, and other
drafting tools I'd never seen before. That day I surrendered my
dream of ever being an architect. I remember it being a sad day,
and for weeks after, I resented Tim Quinn for essentially stealing
my dream. But I moved on.

I imagined around that time that I might become a great bowler. I used to spend hours on Saturday afternoons watching the Pro Bowlers Tour on television. My hero back then was the great Earl Anthony. We had a lot in common, too; both of us wore glasses and were lefties. I joined a league that summer and hung out mostly at the bowling alley. While I never actually owned my own ball (a reality that I still find startling given how much I loved bowling), I did own my own bowling shoes. Every time I began a game, when I stepped up to the line and placed my ball next to my nose and studied the arrow on the lane that would be my mark, I was convinced I was going to bowl a perfect game. And then, when I eventually missed a pin or two (I've never bowled a perfect game), I was certain that I would at least win the game. When I didn't, which was often, I was actually surprised. I never got down on myself, never cussed or had a tantrum. I would simply sit at the desk, score the game, and be genuinely surprised at my defeat.

I imagined, around that time, building and running a home for orphans. The orphanage would be a modern, three-story home with an attic. It would have a huge front porch that looked out onto a finely coiffed front yard, a huge back yard with swing sets, slides, a swimming pool, and enough room to ride bikes. The back fence would abut a creek and acres of wild. My orphanage would have a full-time cook, a television, of course (but the kids couldn't watch it until their homework was done), and enough bedrooms for twenty kids, all of them bunked, as mine was at my home. I love that dream for some reason, enough to remember it forty years later.

As a little boy I imagined being a lawyer, a teacher, an Acapulco cliff diver, an astronaut, a baseball or hockey player depending on the season (I would be a catcher or goalie), and a priest. I imagined winning a million bucks, successfully contacting the souls of the departed, and saving my neighborhood from Communists, Japanese kamikazes, and mole people. I imagined being all these people and doing all these remarkable things before I could read, so it had to be Clark Kent/Superman, Britt Reid/Green Hornet, the

Rifleman, Bruce Wayne/Batman (less so Robin), Hoss and Little Joe, and a hundred others who had instilled in me this sense of my potential greatness and the resilient hope that promised me that as tough as life got, I would win in the end.

Who else would have taught me this? I do not recall my father ever taking me aside and saying to me that I could be anyone I wanted, that I could do great things, the way I'd seen Ward Cleaver, George Mitchell (Dennis the Menace's dad), or Steve Douglas (from *My Three Sons*) take their boys aside and say, in so many words, they were born for important work. What my father taught me back then, he taught by example. From him I learned how to work hard, be a loyal friend, and be generous in my judgments of others. I recall my mother encouraging me on occasion to try new things, to pray for those who got a raw deal (I'm thinking now of the starving children of Biafra when I was a boy), and to believe in God. On the whole, they gave me what I needed from them the most. But I'm beginning to think that it was television (then movies and, finally, books) that gave me my imagination. Or if it was God who blessed me with the capacity to imagine, then television gave me the wherewithal and the permission; television gave me the narrative arc, the structure and form of the story, characters and settings, conflicts and resolutions, and tensions and denouements to live, in my mind, a million possible stories.

With a thousand television episodes under my belt, and a mind formed to believe in the natural course of every story worth living (that is, every story must have a villain—seen or unseen—and a hero, who in the end will win out), I was prepared, I think, for parochial school. I had, of course, heard about Jesus long before I was six years old. I had thumbed through my picture Bible for several years and gotten a pretty good idea about how he looked and what he did. I remember also having a picture book of the saints, which, as I look at it now, might have rivaled television in its influence on me as a child. My favorite saint back then was St. Sebastian, a third-century Christian who in art is often depicted tied to a tree and pierced with arrows. St. Irene apparently healed him after that attempted martyrdom, but he eventually was clubbed to death by Roman soldiers. The Catholic Encyclopedia finds this all historically dubious and not worthy of belief, but I believed it all back then. I wanted to be *that* heroic.

I had, by the time I began first grade, learned my Our Father, Hail Mary, and Glory Be. But even with my fledgling faith, I think I basically understood the story of Jesus as one story among many. Granted, it was a pretty amazing story, and the more I learned about it, the more astonishing it became: tons of villains (too many to list here), a great hero, dizzying plot twists and turns, enough tension and conflict for a lifetime, and best of all, the most unexpected ending imaginable. I ate it up. The thought that I could enter *that* story the way I had entered all those television episodes thrilled me.

By the time I was in second grade I was convinced, actually convinced, that I could be perfect as Jesus was, at least as I understood perfection when I was seven. I began to imagine being a perfect child: always kind and considerate, generous, forgiving, truthful, anticipating other's needs, devoted and obedient to my parents, and always joyful and smiling. I could imagine being this child. I failed at this often, but no one suggested it was going to be easy. In fact, being hard was what made becoming a saint so riveting. I would be tempted, I knew; I would sometimes forget to be perfect and stumble. And then, with a trepidation that eased with each session, I would go to confession, tell Father Stack my sins, get my penance, say my act of contrition (which says in part, "I firmly resolve with the help of thy grace to sin no more and to avoid the near occasion of sin"), be absolved, and leave a new boy.

I believed it was possible to sin no more for two reasons, I think. First, Sister Anna Maria, my second-grade teacher, taught me my act of contrition, and she wouldn't teach me a prayer that wasn't true. And second, I believed it was possible to be perfect because I could *imagine* being perfect. That I wasn't perfect didn't discourage me in the least back then. My story wasn't over yet. I still had plenty of time.

●

I read much more than I watch television these days, and I think that's a good thing. There's nothing like the human imagination unplugged by prose and verse. To keep me planted in terra firma, though, I read the obituary section of the *New York Times* every day. Perhaps it's because I see fewer years ahead of me than behind me, and so I'm drawn more to the stories only obituaries can tell. The other day I read the obituary of the Jewish scientist Rita Levi-Montalcini (I had never heard of her before) who died at the age of 103. She won the Nobel Prize in Physiology or Medicine at the age of seventy-six (along with Stanley Cohen) for discovering the critical chemical tools that the body uses to direct cell growth and build nerve networks. She apparently became initially obsessed with chicken embryos as a young medical doctor in Italy, which she studied in her bedroom during World War II (Mussolini had issued a manifesto barring non-Aryan Italians from having professional careers). From there she went on to unlock one of the great mysteries of human cellular life.

In her autobiography *In Praise of Imperfection*, she wrote, "It is imperfection—not perfection—that is the end result of the program written into that formidably complex engine that is the human brain." The human brain, she thought, seems to have been designed for failure. This struck me as an intriguing thought, one that at first glance seemed counterintuitive. But then I thought, given the role the brain plays, at least part of the time in our lives—to provide a venue for our prodigious imagination—a built-in propensity for failure might serve a larger purpose. I marvel, for instance, that the brain seems to delight in adversity—that it will, if given the chance, rewire itself as best it can to account for a bullet. I'm awestruck at how it adapts to vicissitude, such as aging, a tumor, a stroke, or a virus. And even if we're whittling it down by too much smoking, drinking, or drugging, it's constantly making new connections, always trying to figure out a new way to live, to survive, and to come out, if it can, stronger in the end.

This got me thinking. Imagine for a moment that I had not been discouraged by Tim Quinn and in fact had become, amazingly, an architect. I have no idea what kind of architect I would have become. I hope I would have been a decent one. Or I might have been a terrible architect (that is, mediocre), sitting in my home office (which looks uncannily like Mike Brady's) doodling the night away and imagining what my life could have been if I had had the guts to be the person I always imagined myself being. Either way, I wouldn't be living the life I'm living now, which even with my bad days, I'm actually very happy with. But to get to this life, I've had to endure a whole lot of failure, a whole lot of rewiring, rethinking, and reimagining. That early failure spawned a thousand possible new lives for me, and I eventually chose one that has dropped me off here.

The thing, it seems to me, is to never stop imagining, never stop hoping. My mother told me once, while we were taking a walk on an oncology ward while she was taking her chemotherapy, that when you stop laughing, you die. I agree. But I'll go further. When you stop imagining, *that* sad cul-de-sac spells journey over.

Perhaps this is why, when I am at my worst, I watch *Cops*. On the surface, no one would mistake me for one of those hapless creatures caught in a klieg-lit trap of singular humiliation. I don't watch *Cops* to feel better about myself but because I don't want to actually run (as they almost always try to do) from *my* own shame. I see on television human beings at their worst, hoping at some point I will see them grasping for a scrap, a shard of human dignity. I tell myself (or they tell me), as bad as life gets, you hold on. If everything indeed fails in the end, then my hunch is that hope, that most imaginative of virtues, fails last.

The actor Charles Durning died the other day. I remembered when he played Hewitt, the reluctant deputy on *The High Chaparral*, a television show I watched religiously when I was a kid. I grew to love the characters Durning played over the years on television and in the movies: often gruff, pugnacious, short-tempered, and usually loveable men whose insecurities and self-doubt pulsated just below their skin. But I never really knew the actor until I read his obituary. I learned he was born into poverty, the ninth of ten children. His father, sickened by mustard gas in World War I, died when Charles was a teenager. Never a good student, he dropped out of school and left home at sixteen. Apparently, he thought his mother—a laundress—would fare better with one less mouth to feed. He found work as a farmhand and at other menial jobs in Buffalo. One night, while working at a burlesque nightclub, a frequently drunk comedian failed to show up, so Durning, who had memorized the comic's jokes, persuaded the owner to let him go on. He got laughs, Durning said later, and from that day he was hooked.

As I continued reading, Durning's story became riveting. I learned he enlisted in the army when Pearl Harbor was bombed, survived Omaha Beach on D-Day, a machine gun ambush, and the Battle of the Bulge. In a 1993 interview, he recalled an encounter with a German soldier. "I was crossing a field somewhere in Belgium," he said. "A German soldier ran toward me carrying a bayonet. He couldn't have been more than 14 or 15. I didn't see a soldier. I saw a boy. Even though he was coming at me, I couldn't shoot." The boy attacked him with a knife and stabbed him seven or eight times before Durning could reach for a big rock and slam the boy's head with it over and over until the boy was dead. Durning said afterward he held the boy in his arms and wept.

I read in that obituary that Durning was dogged every day with the fear of failing as an actor, the only job he ever really loved. And yet he kept at it, playing scores of interesting roles on stage (for instance, his Tony Award–winning portrayal of Big Daddy in the 1990 revival of *Cat on a Hot Tin Roof*), screen (my favorite: Jessica Lange's character's father who unwittingly falls in love with

Dustin Hoffman's character masquerading as a woman in *Tootsie*),
and television (among others, a Catholic priest on *Everybody Loves
Raymond*). He worked nearly until the day he died. Way to go,
Charlie, I thought.

The obituary ended with Durning admitting that "there are
many secrets in us, in the depths of our souls, that we don't want
anyone to know about. There's terror and repulsion in us, the terrible spot that we don't talk about. That place that no one knows
about—horrifying things we keep secret. A lot of that is released
through acting." That he included me in his dark admission did
not seem at all out of place.

I thought, *someone's got to put Durning's story on the screen*.
I thought his was probably one of the best stories I'd ever heard.
Durning got life right, I think. I know he pegged mine. More often
than I like to admit, I wake up feeling woefully inadequate to my
life as I know it. And yet, I get up each morning, remarkably, and
wade back into my life, a river of routine, occasional surprises, rare
epiphanies, and sometimes creeping dread. I run around my tiny
patch of the planet for sixteen or seventeen hours and land back
on my couch, where, with a sigh of one sort or another, I cover
my body with a blanket and reach for the remote. I sometimes
fall asleep watching television, carrying into my sleep stories that
occasionally become the stuff of my dreams.

While I'm awake, though, I probably spend too much time
in my head thinking, imagining, and playing out as many possible
scenarios as my taxed brain can handle. Some might read this and
conclude I must not be happy with where I've landed in life or that
I'm not happy with who I am now. Perhaps they are partly right.
I don't know if I'll ever be satisfied with who I am or where I am.
But today I am. Tomorrow? Who knows?

In light of Charles Durning's death, I'm thinking of George
Reeves, the handsome actor who played Superman on television
when I was a boy, who, for whatever reason, put a bullet in his
head a few months before I was born. I can't help thinking now

that in the end, George Reeves, sadly, couldn't imagine a way out of whatever darkness had engulfed him—the way Durning apparently did—that the world had fallen in on him finally one day. He was my boyhood hero. Back then, I probably would have been one of those boys who, upon seeing Reeves on the street, would have run up to him with a BB gun and tried to shoot him. But now, all I see is a tired, middle-aged man who, even with all of his strength, couldn't stop himself from being crushed. He was human, after all.

Notes

Chapter 2: Confession

1. See Steve Pinker, *The Better Angels of Our Nature: Why Violence Has Declined* (New York: Viking, 2011).

Chapter 4: Confirmation

2. Max Brood, ed., *The Diaries of Franz Kafka*, trans. Martin Greenberg with cooperation from Hannah Arendt (New York: Schocken Books, 1949), 214.

3. Ibid., 215, 217.

4. David Foster Wallace, "Laughing with Kafka," *Harper's Magazine*, July 1996, 26.

Chapter 5: Matrimony

5. Mother Teresa, *Come Be My Light: The Private Writings of the Saint of Calcutta*, ed. Brian Kolodiejchuk (New York: Image, 2009), 210.

6. Ibid.

7. James F. Wright, ed., *The Wednesday Letters* (Salt Lake City, UT: Shadow Mountain Press, 2007), accessed January 8, 2014, http://www.thewednesdayletters.com/famous_letters.php.

Patrick Hannon, C.S.C., is a priest of the Congregation of Holy Cross. Raised near Oakland, California, he did his undergraduate work at the University of Portland in Oregon, received his master of divinity at the University of Notre Dame, and holds a master of fine arts in creative writing from Portland State University. Hannon was ordained a priest in 1989 and has, over his twenty-five years as a priest, been a high school English teacher, a high school principal, a parish priest, a rector of a university residence hall, and a campus minister. His essays have appeared in *US Catholic, Portland Magazine, Notre Dame Magazine, The Utne Reader, Best Catholic Writing* and *Gold Man Review*. He is the author of four collections of essays: *Running into the Arms of God, Geography of God's Mercy, The Long Yearning's End,* and *Hearts and Voices*. He ministers and teaches writing at the University of Portland, and he leads parish missions and retreats. He enjoys films, the occasional poker game and microbrew, and spending time with his ever-expanding Irish Catholic family.

Founded in 1865, Ave Maria Press,
a ministry of the Congregation of
Holy Cross, is a Catholic publishing
company that serves the spiritual and
formative needs of the Church and its
schools, institutions, and ministers;
Christian individuals and families; and
others seeking spiritual nourishment.

For a complete listing of titles from

Ave Maria Press

Sorin Books

Forest of Peace

Christian Classics

visit www.avemariapress.com

ave maria press® / Notre Dame, IN 46556
A Ministry of the United States Province of Holy Cross